day drinking

50 cocktails for a mellow buzz | kat odell

workman publishing • new york

For my grandmother Babi,
to whom I owe it all.

Library of Congress Cataloging-in-Publication Data is available.

ISBN 978-0-7611-9320-3

Design by Jean-Marc Troadec

Photography by Nicole Franzen

Drink styling by Kate Schmidt

Prop styling by Sara Abalan

Workman books are available at special discounts when purchased in bulk for premiums and sales promotions as well as for fund-raising or educational use. Special editions or book excerpts can also be created to specification. For details, contact the Special Sales Director at the address below, or send an email to specialmarkets@workman.com.

Workman Publishing Co., Inc.
225 Varick Street
New York, NY 10014-4381
workman.com

Printed in China

First printing March 2017

10 9 8 7 6 5 4 3 2 1

Acknowledgments

I'd like to thank my parents for being my parents and also for introducing me to wine when I was ten. I'd also like to thank them for insisting that I try everything, always.

Thanks to my brother Peter (aka Lulu) for being my cocktail guinea pig.

A mega-huge thanks to my amazing editor, Kylie Foxx McDonald. I feel very fortunate to be under your discerning guidance. Thank you to everyone else at Workman who helped make *Day Drinking* a thing, especially: Jean-Marc Troadec, for the great design; Anne Kerman, for organizing everything (and rescuing my hat); Ying Cheng, Liz Davis, Evan Griffith, Louisa Hager, Thea James, Justin Krasner, Randall Lotowycz, and Kat Millerick for showing their pretty faces; Angela Cherry, Kate Karol, Rachael Mt. Pleasant, Barbara Peragine, Julie Primavera, and James Williamson. Thank you, thank you.

Nicole Franzen (plus Kirsten Francis!), your photos are killer. I'm so grateful that you took on this project. Sara Abalan, thank you for my favorite new tie-dye shirt and for hunting down those vintage vessels. Kate Schmidt, those passionflowers! Thank you for making everything look too pretty to drink.

Big thanks to Stephanie Gomez and Adriana Gomez for hair and makeup; Jamal Birkett; Earlicia Gibb; Steve Stathis, owner of Boarders Surf Shop; and M Apisak from Goodlight Studios.

To the McCarren Hotel gang—especially Ronny Baroody and Stephanie Geyer—thank you for letting us take over your turf for the day. And many thanks to Alexa Mehraban at Tacombi, Fany Gerson at La Tiendita, and the folks at Pulqueria and the Bowery Market.

Thanks to Henry Huang for sticking with me over the years. Rather fittingly, it all began at Coffee Tomo . . .

Thanks to Patty, Nish, Marian, Hannah, and Diane for modeling as my friends herein, and to all my close friends who also allowed me to mildly intoxicate them with the beverages in the book. John, adding milk was indeed the call . . .

And finally, Rebecca. One of my absolute best friends. Reb, I really owe this book to you. Thank you for being open to my gustatory experiments, from college to today. While 101 Bananas and Cristal Light plus vodka may be behind us, I am still down to make you a cocktail with those ingredients any day. :) I love you a million. Thank you.

CONTENTS

HI, I'M KAT!

come day drink with me!

Growing up, I was the kid in school with the smelly lunch. Perhaps it was some super garlicky pesto my dad had made the night before, or it could have been chicken tikka masala from two days past (my dad is of the camp that likes to assert that certain dishes taste better a few days later). Do you know what chicken tikka masala smells like when it's been in a brown paper lunch bag and not refrigerated for hours? I'll spare you the details. Sometimes, all I wanted was to fit in.

But that's what happens when you grow up in America with non-American parents. There's no Kraft macaroni and cheese (a dish I came to love eating at my childhood friend Lauren's house), no chocolate chip cookies (which I didn't start to like until I was about fifteen years old), and no peanut butter and jelly sandwiches on white Wonder bread.

My mom, Vlasta, is from the Czech Republic, and my dad, Andrew, was born in London to Czech parents but grew up in New Jersey. When I was born in New York City, my maternal grandmother, whom I call Babi (that's Czech for "grandmother"), came to take care of me while my parents worked. She's an incredible cook and I grew up preparing countless Czech dishes with her, from cookies and sweet breads (the carby things, not offal) to savory *knedlicky* (dumplings). And it was my grandmother who instilled in me a passion for food and cooking.

My parents were—and still are—very European. And while that was apparent in the food my younger brother, Peter, and I ate growing up, as kids we took for granted all the fresh (never from a box, frequently from my mother's garden) meals we were served. Looking back, it's easy to see how fortunate we were to have parents who embraced a slightly Old World way of life—with family dinner every night composed of made-from-scratch food.

One of the perks of having European parents is their European approach to drinking. As in, they didn't believe that alcohol should be off-limits until age twenty-one. Besides loving food, my dad loves wine—like *really* loves wine—and there was always a bottle (or two!) on the table during dinner. This meant that when I was about ten years old, to my mother's dismay, my dad decided it was time for me to "develop a palate" and introduced me to wine. I clearly remember my first few sips of red wine: I instantaneously hated the sour, tannic liquid. I thought it tasted like vinegar.

Over the years I continued to take sips of wine during dinner, and eventually I started liking the stuff. So, I guess the moral of the story is that I've been drinking since I was ten? Ha, well, no, not really. It's that being exposed to alcohol from a very young age, with my father as my guide, taught me to appreciate beverages for their flavor more than their intoxicating properties.

I was recently talking to my dad about this book and he didn't quite understand the concept of "day drinking." "Who day drinks?" he asked. I thought about it, and my response was, "Everyone." It's true:

Maybe you're having wine at a business lunch, drinking Bellinis at a friend's baby shower, or sipping beers at the beach—all are examples of day drinking. Day drinking often—though not always—takes place on weekends between the hours of noon and 6 p.m., but, hey, if you want to start the mimosas at 10 a.m. on a Tuesday, I'd definitely file that under day drinking, too. Day drinking often takes place outdoors during warm weather (because there's no better way to celebrate the sun than with a mildly boozy drink in hand); that could be on a tropical vacation or simply during spring, summer, or fall months. But day drinking isn't exclusive to warm temps, and can really occur anywhere, during any season, at any time of day.

Now, it's important to distinguish "night drinking" from "day drinking." When you're night drinking, you have a few boozy cocktails, maybe get drunk, then go to sleep. With day drinking, regardless of the setting, you don't want to be gulping strong cocktails because (a) you need to be able to speak without slurring and (b) you probably have responsibilities to attend to later in the day. So, in an effort not to get full-blown wasted, and instead maintain a mellow buzz, the answer here is: low-alcohol libations. And that's where this book comes into play.

I loosely define low-ABV (alcohol by volume) drinks as those containing less than 10 percent booze, which is roughly half the alcohol (or even less) of standard cocktails like a margarita or cosmopolitan. Obviously, that's not an absolute—there are an endless number of tipples in the world with varying amounts of alcohol.

While typical spirits like tequila, vodka, and whiskey contain around 40 percent alcohol by volume, as a point of comparison, wine contains anywhere from 7 to 18 percent alcohol, while beer comes in at around 4 to 9 percent (of course, there are always exceptions). But the point is that "cocktails" as a category don't rely solely on hard liquor. Popular day drinks are often based on beer and wine, which means they are immediately lower in alcohol than their spirit-based counterparts. Take, for example, the beer-based michelada, the prosecco-based Spritz, or even the wine-based sangria. And there are more options to build on from there: fortified wine, hard cider, sake, soju, flavored liqueurs—there's so much alcohol with which to play. In fact, lower-alcohol beverages fare beautifully when combined with other flavors and liquors (even the hard ones).

For the past decade or so, the world of craft cocktails has grown at an exponential pace, and that expansion has been fed in part by the increase in European and Asian alcohols imported into America—amaro, sherry, sake, and soju being just a handful of current examples—and more bottles means more tools for bartenders to get creative. In curating the recipes for this book, I reached out to some of my favorite men and women tending bar from Los Angeles to New York, and asked them to share their best low-ABV recipes. There's so much talent behind the bar these days, with a bevy of bartenders looking to the past for inspiration, while forward-thinking pioneers incorporate ingredients like dry ice and liquid nitrogen.

In the recent past, most low-alcohol cocktails were developed at bars with restricted liquor licenses where bartenders were forced to get creative with beer and wine. But today, fully stocked bars are focusing on low-alcohol tipples just for the hell of it. Because delightful cocktails don't need to come with a hangover the morning after.

It's said that alcoholic beverages enhance food. Beyond food they enhance life. What do you do when you first meet someone? Likely "grab a drink." But it's not always about getting drunk—often it's about enjoying a delicious adult beverage and appreciating the flavor of what you're drinking. The cocktails in this book are tempting lower-alcohol libations prime for afternoon picnics, predinner imbibing, snow days huddled around a fireplace, tailgates and showers, and those times when Uber isn't just a tap away.

COCKTAIL BASICS

Bar Tools, Equipment, and Useful Ingredients

The great thing about learning how to make drinks, as compared with learning how to cook, is that the tools of the trade are relatively inexpensive. Sure, you can score a pricey Japanese gold cocktail shaker on a website like Cocktail Kingdom, but you really don't need one. Which is what I love about drinks. Unlike food (which, come on, I love, too!), where you need at least a set of pots and pans and basic utensils for the process, you can pretty much mix up a drink with a cup and a spoon.

Herein you'll find a guide to the implements, intoxicants, and pantry items that will help you create the concoctions in this book. If you don't have everything on the list, don't sweat it. Again, most any cocktail can be improvised with common kitchen equipment.

Tools and Equipment

Any craft requires tools, and following is a list of gadgets that are helpful in building the drinks in this book. Some will sound familiar, while others may seem obscure. None is absolutely make-or-break essential, but they'll certainly come in handy.

COCKTAIL SHAKER: Cocktail shakers come in many shapes and sizes, but the standard ones you'll find are the Cobbler and the Boston shakers. The Cobbler shaker is generally what bartenders prefer, and it consists of a sturdy mixing glass and a metal tumbler. It's a simple tool that's easy to use: Just place ingredients in the mixing glass, wedge in the metal tumbler to form a tight seal, and shake. The only downside is that as the shaken mixture chills, the two pieces can become difficult to separate.

The Boston shaker, on the other hand, is made up of three pieces that are easy to separate: a metal tumbler, a top with a strainer, and a cap. Simply add the ingredients to the tumbler, secure the top with its built-in strainer (make sure the cap is on, too), and shake.

MIXING GLASS: If you're making a stirred drink, you'll need a mixing glass. This is usually an etched glass that looks like a fancy chemistry class beaker in which you place ice and whatever ingredients you're mixing. (For what it's worth, I've found that stirred drinks are usually boozier than shaken ones. Classic examples are a Manhattan, a gimlet, and martinis that are stirred instead of shaken.)

STRAINER: Two basic cocktail strainers exist: the Hawthorne strainer and the julep strainer. You'll usually see a bartender

a note on single- and double-straining

Most of the recipes in this book call for a single strain—meaning you pour the cocktail through the Hawthorne or julep strainer and straight into the glass—but you may come across one that calls for a second strain. The idea behind that is to doubly ensure that all solids are separated from the liquid for a super smooth texture. When a recipe calls for a double strain, you'll affix a Hawthorne to your cocktail shaker, position a fine-mesh sieve over your vessel of choice, and pour the drink through it. Double whammy.

straining a cocktail from a tin with a Hawthorne strainer, while the julep is commonly used to strain a drink from a mixing glass. The logic here is simple enough: The Hawthorne fits better to a tin and the julep to a mixing glass. (My personal preference is the Hawthorne-and-tin combo.) When using a julep strainer, you'll want to wedge it into the glass bowl-side down and hold it steady with your forefinger, so it "catches" the ice as you pour the drink.

JIGGER: What cups and measuring spoons are to cooking, the jigger is to cocktails. It's the standard hourglass-shaped metal tool used to measure ounces, usually 1½ ounces (1 jigger) on one end and ¾ ounce (half a jigger) on the other. These implements can vary in size, though, so just make sure to double-check your jigger's capacity.

AT LEFT: 1 Microplane grater **2** Hawthorne strainer **3** peeler **4 & 7** muddlers **5** bar spoon **6** bottle opener **8** Lewis bag and mallet **9** citrus juicer **10** cutting boards **11** OXO Mini Angled Measuring Cup **12** paring knife **13** chef's knife **14** fine-mesh sieve **15** measuring spoons **16** jigger **17** julep strainer

MEASURING CUP: Most of the recipes in this book use a jigger, mentioned earlier, but some of the syrups and large-format drinks call for cups as a form of measurement. Two-cup capacity liquid measuring cups are especially useful here.

The syrup recipes usually yield more syrup than needed for one drink, so if you want to make half, a quarter, or even an eighth of a recipe, OXO's Mini Angled Measuring Cup is an awesome tool (it can even measure out small amounts like $\frac{1}{16}$ of an ounce). It also shows measurements in tablespoons and milliliters.

MEASURING SPOONS: Some of the recipes call for both ounce measurements and standard U.S. measures: teaspoons and tablespoons. It's useful to know that 1 ounce equals 2 tablespoons in case you (a) can't find a jigger or (b) want to scale a drink yield up or down. (For more bar tool equivalencies, see the table on page 229.)

BAR SPOON: Several different types of bar spoons exist, but they generally serve the same purpose—to mix stirred cocktails. They also function as a tool to measure ingredients: 1 bar spoon equals about 1 teaspoon.

MUDDLER: You need one of these! While you can improvise if you don't have certain bar tools—like a cocktail shaker or a bar spoon—this is one tool that I strongly suggest acquiring (and it's cheap to boot). A muddler to a mixing glass or cocktail tin is like a pestle to a mortar. It breaks down fruit and herbs and helps infuse flavors in a cocktail. Muddlers come in all shapes and sizes—some are wooden, and others are metal. Personally, I like a simple, unvarnished wooden muddler that's about 1 inch in diameter. It's easy to hold, especially when breaking down firm ingredients like melon or tomatoes.

KNIVES: The cocktails in this book call for a variety of fruits and vegetables, and having a large and small knife will help you prep them. A paring knife is great for peeling certain ingredients like apples and pears, and a chef's knife is great for chopping and slicing.

FRUIT PEELER: It's helpful to have a standard vegetable peeler to remove strips of zest or peel the skin from citrus fruits. I've found that a peeler removes skin more easily and in a more uniform shape than a paring knife.

MICROPLANE GRATER: If you don't have a Microplane, I urge you to get a zester-grater combo. It's the ideal tool for finely grating citrus zest, and also for freshly grating ingredients like whole nutmeg and knobs of ginger.

CUTTING BOARD: Don't ruin your countertop—make sure to break out a wooden or plastic cutting board to prevent knife marks and citrus juice from damaging counters.

CITRUS JUICER: While you can buy a citrus juicer inexpensively, at home I simply use a fork. Why complicate things? It can be useful, however, when juicing *lots* of citrus.

FINE-MESH SIEVE: A few of the recipes in this book call for double-straining drinks or straining syrups or juice, but you'll most often use this for citrus. If you're using fresh lemon or lime juice in your drinks (and I'd really advise you to do so), pass the juice through a sieve to separate out seeds and bigger clumps of pulp. A small sieve that fits the rim of a glass—a tea strainer works well—is ideal.

POTS AND PANS: These kitchen workhorses are useful for making simple syrup and the like. I'm a fan of stainless steel cookware because nonstick emits toxic fumes when overheated.

STORAGE CONTAINERS: Bottles and jars, either plastic or glass, in a range of sizes with tight-fitting lids, are great to have around at home to store extra syrups and fresh juices. And, in a pinch, a 12- or 16-ounce jar can serve as a cocktail shaker.

ELECTRIC JUICER: You don't need a juicer to make the recipes in this book, but if you have one, it will definitely come in handy. And the good news is that there are now electric juicers on the market for less than $100. (Bonus: You can use your juicer to make delicious and healthful nonalcoholic drinks, too—including the mocktails in "Buzz-Free Beverages.") If a home juicer isn't in the cards, try visiting a local juice press or a market like Whole Foods, which may have an on-site juice bar that will squeeze or press the fresh stuff for you on the spot.

BLENDER: You can get away with making most drinks in this book without a blender (with the exception of the really excellent tiki-inspired cocktail, the Regents Royale, on page 155, which requires one). I use a Vitamix, and if you have one, or another kind of high-power blender, that's great. But for the sake of these recipes, feel free to use a more basic model (which can be a handy stand-in for a juicer; see the hack on page 15).

the juice on juice Although I'm a believer that fresh is best when it comes to juice, there are some times when it's more important to seek out the fresh stuff than others. For example, quality packaged orange and grapefruit juices are readily accessible and can easily be swapped in for fresh. This is not so for lemon or lime juice. Those juices, when sold in those plastic lemon- or lime-shaped containers or from concentrate, have an unnatural flavor that will ruin your drink. And come on—you can find fresh lemons and limes everywhere. There's no excuse for not juicing your own.

When sourcing juices, I generally stay away from concentrates. They have flavors that are the furthest from fresh-tasting. Next, I like to look for juices with the shortest shelf life; that usually means they're the least manipulated (many store-bought juices use heat pasteurization to extend shelf life) and will taste the most natural.

For fresh vegetable and noncitrus fruit juices, it's ideal to have a juicer on hand. But if you don't, sourcing from a juice bar is an excellent alternative (see page 14). And if that's not an option, then you can MacGyver your own juicer with a basic blender. Simply blend the produce until it becomes a mushy pulp, then use the back of a wooden spoon to press it through cheesecloth or a fine-mesh sieve. You can use the juice in your cocktail and reserve the pulp for a yogurt or cereal topping.

Glassware

A glass is functional beyond serving as a vessel that contains a beverage—the shape of a glass will affect a drink's smell, temperature, and taste. While restaurants stock a wide variety of glassware, it's not imperative to own 30 different kinds (though it is nice!). I find the following to be the most useful types: Champagne flute (for a Champagne cocktail, Kir Royale, Bellini mimosa); coupe glass (for a Champagne cocktail, daiquiri, martini); Collins or highball glass (for a fizz, gin and tonic, Moscow mule); old-fashioned or rocks glass (for a Negroni, an old-fashioned); tea cup or mug (for Irish coffee, hot toddy, warm punch); wineglass (for wine, wine-based cocktails like sangria).

How to Do This and That

Unlike cooking, most bar techniques can be mastered in a jiff. All you really need is a bit of basic knowledge and some simple tools.

Muddle

Using what looks like a small wooden or metal baseball bat, this is a way of breaking up fruit and herbs to release flavor and aromatics. It's a pretty straightforward technique: Basically you

---

AT LEFT: **1** Irish coffee mug **2** tea cup **3** pint glass **4** highball glass **5** rocks glass **6** Boston shaker **7** Cobbler shaker **8 & 9** mixing glasses **10** julep cup **11** coupe glass **12** martini glass **13** Nick and Nora glass **14** Champagne flute **15 & 16** wineglasses **17** tulip-shape glass **18** pitcher **19** punch bowl and ladle **20** punch glasses

want to smash and twist your muddler in the bottom of a cocktail tin or mixing glass to pulverize your ingredients.

Shaken or Stirred?

The age-old debate! Drinks are either shaken (in a cocktail shaker) or stirred (in a mixing glass). Experts, however, disagree on whether certain cocktails, like the martini, absolutely must be shaken or stirred. A general rule of thumb: Shake a drink when it contains fruit juice, eggs, dairy, sour mix, or cream liqueurs, such as Into the Woods (page 205). The idea here is to make sure all ingredients are aggressively incorporated. When shaking with a tin, shake until your ice is broken up and the outside of the tin becomes frosty, about 15 seconds (unless otherwise directed). While the size of the ice doesn't really matter, I personally like to use standard 1-inch cubes.

Meanwhile, when a drink contains only translucent booze, like the Sakura Martini (page 173), you'll want to stir its ingredients in a mixing glass filled two-thirds full with ice cubes for about 1 minute.

Dry Shake

When a cocktail contains egg—such as a pisco sour or Ramos gin fizz or, in the case of this book, the Cynar Flip (page 65)— the ingredients need to be emulsified in the shaker before the ice is added. (A dry shake is "dry" because there's no ice.) To do this, add all the ingredients to a cocktail shaker—but hold the ice!—and vigorously shake the mixture for 30 seconds. Then add the ice and shake again for another 30 seconds to chill the mixture and dilute it.

Booze Basics

I n the following pages, you'll find recipes that call predominantly for low-alcohol bases. Some of these may be unfamiliar, like vermouth and sherry, but others you'll know well, like wine and beer. Occasionally, a recipe will call for a full-proof spirit, but only a minimal amount, which keeps the cocktail's proof around or below 20 percent.

With producers releasing new potables seemingly daily, there's a near-infinite number of booze bottles out there. I don't expect you to know them all—here's some basic info to get you situated.

Amaro

Amaro, the Italian word for "bitter," is a class of bittersweet *aperitivi* and *digestivi* (Italian for "aperitifs" and "digestifs," respectively) that are flavored with botanicals from the region in which the liqueur was produced. Consumed throughout Europe, amari are especially popular in Italy, and the category is quickly growing in the United States as well. While different amari channel different levels of bittersweet, they all pack an herbaceousness. Some amari are characterized by one main flavor, like Cynar, for example, which contains artichoke. Meanwhile, Averna and Aperol both taste of orange, while Campari tastes of bitter orange. If you ever want to impress a bartender, just walk up to a bar and order a shot of Fernet-Branca. The hardcore bitter, minty-mouthwash-tasting liqueur is the unofficial bartenders' shot.

fortified and aromatized wines: what's what? A fortified wine is a wine that's bolstered by the addition of a high-proof liquor, commonly a neutral grape spirit like a clear brandy. Fortified wines can be dry or sweet, and they're often consumed before dinner or after dinner, as an aperitif or digestif. Popular examples include sherry (see below), port (a Portuguese dessert wine that's typically red in color, and rich and sweet), Madeira (wines that range from dry to sweet and are produced on Portugal's Madeira Islands), and marsala (wines made in a range of sweetness levels in Marsala, Sicily).

Wines that are fortified with a high-proof spirit and infused with a medley of botanicals fall under the category of aromatized wines, the most well known being vermouth. Aromatized wines can be further classified based on the primary botanical flavoring the liquor. For example, vermouths incorporate wormwood as the main bittering agent, quinquinas and chinatos call for quinine (the same ingredient that gives tonic its bitter flavor) from cinchona bark, and Americanos utilize gentian (a bitter root).

Sherry

A fortified wine produced in the three Andalusian towns of Jerez de la Frontera, El Puerto de Santa María, and Sanlúcar de Barrameda, sherry is made in a variety of styles from dry to sweet, saline to fruity, and contains anywhere from 15 to more than 20 percent ABV. The cocktails in this book use only a handful of the styles, as listed below from dry to sweet.

FINO: This is the driest sherry style and is made with the Palomino grape. Fino sherries are white wines that age under a layer of yeast called *flor*, which protects the wine from oxidation. Fino sherry can have a saline, briny flavor.

MANZANILLA: Manzanilla sherry is basically the same as fino sherry except that it must be produced in the town of Sanlúcar de Barrameda, which is right along the ocean. To me, Manzanilla sherry tastes of ocean water in the best possible way.

AMONTILLADO: I love this style of aged sherry for its deep, nutty, umami flavor. It is a partially oxidized style, meaning that the wine isn't entirely protected by the *flor*. Unlike fino and Manzanilla sherries, which both look like white wine, amontillado has a deep brown hue.

PALO CORTADO: Centuries ago, winemakers didn't fully understand how to make Palo Cortado–style sherry. Sometimes a batch of wine on its way to becoming an amontillado (meaning it started as a fino but then lost its *flor*) would mysteriously become an even richer version of itself, with no rhyme or reason. Because of this, Palo Cortado has always been the rarest style of sherry. True Palo Cortado is still somewhat of a mystery, though it can also be made by blending amontillado with oloroso sherry (darker and nuttier than amontillado).

PEDRO XIMÉNEZ (PX): Named after the grape itself, Pedro Ximénez is a sweet sherry made from grapes that are usually dried in the sun to concentrate their flavor. PX sherry can be as viscous as maple syrup, with a deep, intense raisin flavor.

aperitif or digestif? Don't know the difference? An aperitif is any alcoholic beverage customarily consumed before dinner to stimulate one's appetite. Typically lower in sugar and alcohol than a digestif—which is consumed after a meal to aid in digestion—common aperitifs include vermouth, sherry, Campari, and Aperol. Popular digestif liqueurs include brandy, port, and fernet, as well as some more obscure drinks like lemony limoncello and herbal Chartreuse.

Vermouth

Vermouth is a category of aromatized, fortified aperitif wines, meaning vermouths start with a wine base that's macerated with botanicals and then fortified with a spirit (often unaged brandy). Vermouth can be sipped solo, or incorporated into many cocktails beyond the martini. The styles of vermouth you'll most commonly encounter are dry or sweet; however, vermouth is also categorized by its color, like red, white, or even rosé vermouth. In general, red vermouth is sweet. White vermouth can be either dry or sweet; however, if it's not specifically labeled as dry, then you can assume it's sweet. Rosé vermouth is like a cross between the two—its sweetness level falls somewhere in the middle.

Beer

Just like the world of craft cocktails, the world of craft beer has exploded in the past decade, and the United States has emerged as a leader in this beverage category. Going beyond traditional lagers and ales, brews from coast to coast are made with everything from Pop Rocks to Thai basil, yielding a rainbow of drinks with ingredients common and unsung. It wouldn't really be fair to say that one beer is better than another for a low-ABV drink, because ultimately it depends on the other ingredients that mingle with it. But as a general rule of thumb, I use the following pairings/guidelines:

- The fresh, bitter notes in IPAs work well with spice (chiles), citrus (grapefruit, orange), and tropical fruit (pineapple, kiwi). This beer style also pairs with earthy liquors like mezcal and tequila.

- The rich flavors found in dark stouts and barrel-aged beers make this style a match for brown spirits like whiskey.

- Thanks to their fruity off-flavors (esters), Belgian-style beers work well in fruitier cocktails.

- The peppery, gingery, lemony flavors in saison beers work well in cocktails that contain similar flavor profiles.

- The most classic light lager pairing just might be Corona Extra in a michelada. But light lagers also work with spirits like peaty Islay Scotch.

- The maltiness found in brown ales nicely complements bourbon-based drinks.

Hard Cider

Hard cider is made throughout the world, specifically in regions like Spain's Basque Country, where it's called *sidra*; Brittany, France, where it's called *cidre*; and in both England and the United States, where it's called, well, cider. Cider is made from the fermented juice of apples grown specifically for cider making, and based on where in the world it's made, it takes on a range of flavors from sweet to funky. While cider varies in ABV, generally it's about as strong as beer. Again, like beer, different ciders will fare well in different cocktails, simply based on the other ingredients incorporated. Personally, because I am keen on funky flavors, I like Basque-style cider, which can be both sour and barnyardy.

Sake

Sake is a type of Japanese wine made from rice. Depending on the type of sake—junmai, ginjo, daiginjo—rice grains are polished to remove impurities, so the more a grain is polished, supposedly the more pure a sake will taste. Once the rice grains are polished, they enter the sake brewing process. Just like grape wine, sake can be dry or sweet. For the purpose of the cocktails in this book, any dry, floral sake will work.

Fruit and Other Liqueurs

MARASCHINO: Originally produced in what's now Croatia, maraschino, now made in Italy, is a clear, semi-dry, cherry-almond–flavored liqueur made from the fruit and pit of the marasca cherry. The cherries are distilled, and sugar is added to sweeten the distillate, at which point the liqueur is aged, filtered, then bottled. Several brands make a maraschino liqueur, but the one you're most likely to find at a local liquor store and the one I'd recommend is by Luxardo.

CRÈME DE CASSIS: The flavoring component in the classic French aperitif known as the Kir Royale (page 100), crème de cassis is a syrupy-sweet Burgundian black currant liqueur.

ST-GERMAIN: St-Germain is also a syrupy-sweet liqueur flavored with the blossoms of elderflowers that grow in the French Alps.

High-Proof Alcohols

High-proof alcohols are your typical vodka, gin, whiskey, tequila, rum, mezcal—all those spirits that clock in at about 40 percent ABV or 80 proof. Although you might think there's no room for these guys in a day drinker's low-ABV world, not so. The basic idea behind adding full-proof spirits is to use less of them, usually ½ or ¼ ounce. For spirits other than vodka, these full-proof liquors will still add a subtle flavor to a cocktail.

The Day Drinker's Pantry

Simple Syrups and Their Kin

Simple syrup is a staple for any bar. It's made from water and sugar in equal parts. But the great thing about this sweetener is that you can add any other flavors—like strawberries and basil—and stash that syrup in your fridge, allowing you to quickly build a fruit drink without having to break out any fresh fruit. A basic simple syrup will keep in your fridge for about a month, but if you add a tablespoon of vodka to the batch, you'll extend its life for up to three months (and won't increase its ABV all that much).

SIMPLE SYRUP

This is your most basic sugar syrup. MAKES 1½ CUPS

1 cup water
1 cup sugar

HEAT THE WATER IN A small saucepan over low heat until it simmers, about 3 minutes. Add the sugar and remove the pan from the heat. Stir to dissolve the sugar and allow the mixture to cool to room temperature before using. Transfer any leftover syrup to an airtight container and refrigerate.

Simple Syrup will keep, covered and refrigerated, for 1 month.

RICH SIMPLE SYRUP

Rich simple syrup is twice as sweet as regular simple syrup, which means you need less in a cocktail. MAKES 2 CUPS

1 cup water
2 cups sugar

HEAT THE WATER IN A small saucepan over low heat until it simmers, about 3 minutes. Add the sugar and remove the pan from the heat. Stir to dissolve the sugar and allow the mixture to cool to room temperature before using. Transfer any leftover syrup to an airtight container and refrigerate.

Rich Simple Syrup will keep, covered and refrigerated, for 1 month.

DEMERARA SYRUP

Demerara sugar is light brown in color, has larger grains than white sugar, and comes from Guyana. As compared with white sugar, it carries more of a caramel flavor. **MAKES 1½ CUPS**

1 cup water
1 cup demerara sugar

HEAT THE WATER IN A small saucepan over low heat until it simmers, about 3 minutes. Add the sugar and remove the pan from the heat. Stir to dissolve the sugar and allow the mixture to cool to room temperature before using. Transfer any leftover syrup to an airtight container and refrigerate.

Demerara Syrup will keep, covered and refrigerated, for 1 month.

HONEY SYRUP

Honey syrup is just like simple syrup, but it's made with honey in place of sugar. Naturally, it will add the subtle flavor of honey to a drink. While there are many types of honey, a good all-purpose one to use is clover honey. I am also keen on the floral notes in orange blossom honey. Both are readily available at the supermarket. **MAKES 2 CUPS**

1 cup honey
1 cup warm water

COMBINE THE HONEY AND WARM water in a bowl and stir until blended. Allow the syrup to cool to room temperature before using. Transfer any leftover syrup to an airtight container and refrigerate.

Honey Syrup will keep, covered and refrigerated, for several weeks.

. . . .

RICH HONEY SYRUP

Similar to rich simple syrup, rich honey syrup is also built from a ratio of two parts honey to one part water. **MAKES 1½ CUPS**

½ cup warm water
1 cup honey

COMBINE THE HONEY AND WARM water in a bowl and stir until blended. Allow the syrup to cool to room temperature before using. Transfer any leftover syrup to an airtight container and refrigerate.

Rich Honey Syrup will keep, covered and refrigerated, for several weeks.

. . . .

ORGEAT SYRUP

Orgeat is a delicious nutty-flavored syrup made from toasted almonds. It can be used in place of simple syrup. Although this orgeat contains some alcohol, the amount is negligible—especially when considering the overall volume of the syrup. **MAKES 1¼ CUPS**

2 cups raw almonds, chopped
1½ cups sugar
1¼ cups water
1 teaspoon orange-flower water
1 ounce brandy

1 Preheat the oven to 375°F.

2 Place the almonds on a rimmed baking sheet and bake until golden brown, about 4 minutes. Let cool.

3 Transfer the almonds to a food processor and process until finely ground. Set aside.

4 Combine the sugar and water in a small saucepan over medium-high heat, stirring to dissolve the sugar, about 3 minutes. Reduce the heat to medium-low and stir in the ground almonds. Bring the mixture to a boil, then remove it from the heat. Cover and let the mixture steep, at least 3 hours and up to 8 hours.

5 Stretch a layer of cheesecloth over the mouth of a large glass jar and strain the nut mixture through it, discarding the solids. Add the orange-flower water and brandy, cover, and shake to incorporate.

Orgeat Syrup will keep, covered and refrigerated, for about 2 weeks.

Ice

Many bartenders wax poetic on the importance of ice in a cocktail, and they're right. Think about it. There's ice in most cocktails, and as that ice melts, it's not only going to dilute your drink, but if the ice isn't fresh, it will add unwanted flavor to your cocktail. Ever had a drink with ice that tastes like a stale freezer? Not good. So it's important to have fresh ice on hand.

MAKING ICE AND ICE SHAPES: There's an endless supply of ice molds in all shapes and sizes on the market now, from massive cubes to sleek cylinders, from soccer balls to ocean animals . . . there's pretty much an ice mold for every taste. But for *Day Drinking* recipes, shape doesn't really matter—all you really need are standard (1-inch) cubes, large (2-inch) cubes, crushed ice (see box), and occasionally a large punch bowl ring (which you can make by freezing water in a Bundt pan). And if push comes to shove, you can really get away with just cubes.

You'll notice that some ice molds are made of hard plastic (think of the trays that came with your fridge), while others are made from flexible silicone. For standard-size cubes, I prefer the traditional hard plastic molds because the ice is much easier to remove from the tray. I've found that small squares in the silicone molds require a fair amount of prying and your fingers will be partially frozen by the end. When you're looking to make ice in atypical shapes or sizes (including the bigger cubes that are currently popular), silicone molds are the way to go. You can find a wide array of choices online.

MAKING FLOWER ICE CUBES: It's easy to create colorful floral cubes to give your drink an extra flourish. Arrange assorted small edible flowers facedown in the bottom of each mold of an ice

lewis bag/mallet This is a set of tools (a small canvas bag and what looks like a wooden hammer) that will help you turn regular ice cubes into crushed ice for drinks like a julep. You can get them online for about $25, but if you don't feel like investing the time or money, here's an easy hack: Grab a kitchen towel, lay it out flat, place your ice in the center, and gather the sides of the towel up around it so the ice is covered and positioned in the middle. Next, find a hard surface (I use the tile floor in my bathroom) and whack the bundle of ice about three or four times against it to break up the cubes. Works like a charm. The ice pieces won't be entirely uniform, but they'll certainly be better than standard cubes in a drink that calls for crushed.

cube tray. Carefully pour distilled water (or water that you've boiled and let cool—this will ensure crystal clear ice) over the flowers to fill each ice cube mold halfway. Freeze the cubes until solid, about 10 hours. Add the remaining distilled or boiled water to fill each cube completely. Freeze again until solid, and reserve in the freezer until ready to use.

Bitters

Bartenders sometimes describe bitters as the salt and pepper of the bar world, but I've also heard a bartender call the salt and pepper of the bar world, well, salt and pepper. The general idea behind bitters is that they add complexity to a drink, enhancing and balancing its ingredients. Though made in an endless combination of flavors, bitters start with a base of high-proof alcohol in which botanicals are infused. The recipes in this book call for a variety of bitters, from Mexican mole–scented to the classic Angostura. If you're looking to stock just the basics, I'd suggest Angostura, Peychaud's, and an orange-flavored bitter, like Regans' Orange Bitters No. 6. You can buy these at most liquor stores and online.

Garnishes

I love cocktail garnishes and accessories. From gold straws to carved fruit to temporary tattoos (no joke, one New York restaurant serves a drink that comes with a temporary tattoo and a friendship bracelet!), bartenders have really upped their garnish game. Most of the recipes in this book involve garnishes, but not all. A couple of notes: (1) If you don't have the extra ingredients or "flair" needed to garnish a drink, leave them out—a garnish rarely affects a cocktail's flavor. (2) If you'd like to get creative and invent your own garnishes for these drinks, please do!

GARNISH PREP: For the most part, I like to make my garnishes right before they land on a drink. For example, if you're adding a 2-inch swatch of citrus zest (a popular cocktail addition), you'll want the oils from the peel to add a hint of flavor to the cocktail; if you prep those in advance, then the skin will dry out. Sometimes you'll add fresh herbs to a cocktail, which is an easy last-minute accent because all you need to do is stick a sprig or leaf in a drink, *et voilà*.

IF YOU'RE THROWING A PARTY: My favorite low-effort-but-still-beautiful party garnish is unsprayed edible flowers, like violets, rose petals, and basil blossoms. If you're throwing a fête, you want to be able to spend time with your guests and not be stuck in the kitchen cooking and mixing drinks the whole time. So, you'll want to prebatch your cocktails and choose simple but pretty garnishes. Edible flowers fancy up any drink, making them highly versatile. They look beautiful in punches; you can just lay them atop the surface before serving. Super easy. Another party-ready garnish idea is frozen fruit. Think grapes, strawberries, blackberries . . . really anything small works. You can also freeze these, as well as those edible flowers, into ice cubes (see page 30).

Aside from garnishes that are just for show—like flowers or citrus peels—if you're adding fruit, vegetables, or another edible like olives, you'll want that to echo the main ingredients in the cocktail.

SUMMER LOVIN'
Light Drinks for Hot Days

Certain drinks were built for hot weather imbibing. While the English reach for fruity Pimm's to build the country's traditional low-alcohol sipper, no trip to Mexico would be complete without a proper michelada: a mix of Mexican beer, lime juice, tomato juice, and myriad spices and sauces like Tajín, Worcestershire, chile, and more. But as craft cocktail culture continues to proliferate in the United States, enterprising bartenders are moving past the classics and adding their own spin to low-alcohol drinks. Especially popular right now are wine- (think sherry and vermouth), beer-, and cider-based beverages, sometimes with a nod to tiki, other times spiked with coffee. You'll notice that many cocktails are carbonated—because the bubbles in beer and cider serve as a swift refresher, cutting right through a hot summer day.

The drinks in this chapter have a light body, often with a fruity flavor profile, and overall are a welcome solution to a hot, hot day. Herein, a mix of fresh flavors, both classic and new (coffee and yuzu, anyone?!), some with bubbles, some without.

lady
ROGERS

FROM **PAMELA WIZNITZER** OF **SEAMSTRESS, NEW YORK CITY**

Named after the performer Ginger Rogers, the star of this drink is the ginger liqueur, which adds a spicy kick to its Lillet base. I am a total sucker for Lillet-based drinks. The French aromatized wine tastes like summer to me. It's light, just sweet enough, and has a faint scent of flowers. This drink is a low-ABV take on a Moscow mule—traditionally vodka mixed with dry ginger beer—with a floral foundation of Lillet. **MAKES 1**

1½ ounces Lillet Blanc (see box, page 38)

¾ ounce ginger liqueur, such as Canton

¾ ounce fresh lime juice

¼ ounce Rich Honey Syrup (page 28)

Soda water

Lime wheel, for garnish

Fill a highball glass three-quarters full with ice cubes. Add the Lillet, ginger liqueur, lime juice, and syrup. Top with soda water. Stir gently and garnish with the lime wheel.

meet lillet Lillet is a flowery French aromatized wine that's made from a blend of wine and fruit liqueurs, yielding a mildly sweet, elegant drink. The Lady Rogers calls for Lillet Blanc, but note that Lillet is made in two other colors: Rouge (red) and Rosé. The Blanc and Rosé are made from a Semillon wine base, while the Rouge begins with Merlot.

Lillet is great on its own over ice, but it's also a popular cocktail addition. Here are some of my favorite and supremely simple takes on it:

- Lillet Blanc over ice, garnished with cucumber and lemon slices, and topped with soda water—a beautiful summer refresher.

- Lillet Blanc over ice with a splash of dry sparkling wine and an orange slice.

- Lillet Rouge served in a wineglass with one ice cube.

the world's
best
PIMM'S
CUP

FROM **NAREN YOUNG** OF **DANTE, NEW YORK CITY**

I have a friend in Los Angeles who, one day after noticing a cocktail photo I had posted on Instagram, hashtagged "#drinkswithsnacks." Perhaps it's my affinity for food, but I love a good cocktail that comes with a snack. This recipe, a classic Pimm's Cup, is the ultimate fruit salad in drink form. And what's especially great about this drink, aside from its aesthetic appeal, is that it's entirely customizable with whatever seasonal fruit you have on hand. Toss in some berries, grapes, or even cubed watermelon. Just don't forget the cucumber!

Pimm's is an English herbal aperitif originally released in the mid-nineteenth century. There are actually six Pimm's formulas, each based on a different spirit and flavors, which is where the "No.1" comes into play. The first of the Pimm's—No. 1, appropriately—is based on gin and imbued with fruit peels and herbs like bitter quinine (the same flavoring used in tonic). Naren Young's take on the cocktail features an unusual star anise tincture. You don't have to make the tincture, but it adds an intriguing, ineffable spice. And it's very easy to make—you just need to plan ahead. **MAKES 1**

· ·

1½ ounces Pimm's No.1

½ ounce floral gin, such as Hendrick's

½ ounce dry curaçao, such as Pierre Ferrand

¼ ounce fresh lemon juice

5 drops Star Anise Tincture (recipe follows; optional)

About 2 ounces ginger beer, such as Fever-Tree, chilled

Thinly sliced cucumbers, mint sprigs, and assorted fresh fruit and veggies, such as raspberries, currants, and watermelon radish, for garnish

· ·

Combine the Pimm's, gin, curaçao, lemon juice, and star anise tincture (if using) in a wineglass and stir to blend. Top with ginger beer. Garnish frivolously with seasonal fresh fruit and sprigs of mint. Cucumber is a must!

PRO TIPS

- Sub in a splash of chilled Champagne or sparkling wine for the ginger beer to make a Pimm's Royale.
- During colder months swap a smoky Scotch for the gin to make a winter-friendly Pimm's Cup.

star anise
TINCTURE

makes 6 ounces

---

6 ounces vodka

5 or 6 star anise pods

PLACE THE VODKA IN A glass jar or bottle, add the anise pods, and steep for 5 days. Strain out the anise pods and use a funnel to pour the tincture into a small bottle. Use an eyedropper for easy measuring. The tincture will keep, covered in a cool, dry, dark place, indefinitely.

spiked
ICED TEA

And I am not talking about the stuff from Long Island. This cleaner, lower-proof version gives new purpose to Pimm's beyond the usual Cup (see page 39). Iced tea in general serves as a pretty malleable base for myriad liquors, and if you pick a sweetened type of booze, then you don't even need to add honey. **MAKES 1**

....

6 ounces brewed black tea (I like Earl Grey here), chilled

3 ounces Pimm's No. 1

¼ ounce fresh lemon juice

½ ounce honey

....

Fill a Collins glass with ice cubes. Add the tea, Pimm's, lemon juice, and honey, and stir well to combine.

variations

- If you find yourself with a bottle of the lemony Italian liqueur limoncello, add 1 ounce of the liqueur to 6 ounces chilled, unsweetened black tea for a taste of coastal southern Italy.
- Those with sweet red or white vermouth at home can add a floral and herbal hit with 3 ounces vermouth to 6 ounces chilled, unsweetened black tea.
- Pedro Ximénez sherry adds a raisiny touch to tea. Go with 2 ounces sherry plus ⅛ ounce fresh lemon juice to 6 ounces chilled, unsweetened black tea.
- For an orangey twist, mix 1 ounce dry curaçao and ⅛ ounce fresh lemon juice with 6 ounces chilled, unsweetened black tea.

ROSÉ all day

FROM **DEVON ESPINOSA** OF **THE CHURCH KEY, LOS ANGELES**

"**S**ummer in a cup." That's what one of my friends calls this drink. It is the ultimate pool-perfect libation to sip on a hot day. Strawberries, rosé, and mild carbonation yield a refreshing, barely sweet tipple. The hit of Aperol adds complexity to the drink thanks to the liqueur's bittersweet orange flavor.

This recipe also scales up easily, making it an awesome party option served in a pitcher or punch bowl. Just multiply each ingredient by the number of guests. If making a large batch, skip muddling the strawberries and instead cut them up and macerate them in the rosé, which can be kept chilled in the fridge for a few hours. You can strain out the strawberries or leave them in (I like to keep them as a snack and for visual appeal), then stir in the remaining ingredients. Add the ice to each glass when serving. **MAKES 1**

2 strawberries, hulled

4 ounces rosé wine, chilled

1 ounce Aperol

½ ounce fresh lemon juice

Soda water, chilled

Muddle the strawberries in a mixing glass or cocktail shaker. Add the rosé, Aperol, and lemon juice, and stir to incorporate. Pour into a wineglass, add a handful of ice cubes, and top with a splash of soda water.

ORCHARD

75

FROM **NICK DUBLE** OF **ATERA, NEW YORK CITY**

T he beauty of this cocktail lies in its inherent apple-meets-almond flavor, with an underlying savory funkiness imparted by the hard cider. In this drink, I like French cider from the Normandy region because it has a very dry, farmhouse-y character to it, which serves to balance out any sweetness in the drink. If you must use a different type of hard cider, the recipe will still work but the drink's flavor will change. **MAKES 1**

1½ ounces Calvados (see box)

¾ ounce fresh lemon juice

¾ ounce Almond Syrup (recipe follows)

Pinch salt

3 ounces dry French hard apple cider, such as Etienne Dupont Cidre Bouché, chilled

2 slices apple or pear, for garnish

1 Fill a stemmed beer glass with crushed ice.

2 Fill a cocktail shaker halfway with ice cubes. Add the Calvados, lemon juice, almond syrup, and salt, cover, and shake to chill and mix ingredients, about 20 seconds. Add the cider to the shaker and stir to incorporate.

3 Strain the cocktail into the glass. Garnish with the apple slices.

almond SYRUP

makes about 1 cup

---

1 cup plain, unsweetened almond milk

1 cup sugar

COMBINE THE ALMOND MILK AND sugar in a blender and process until the sugar has fully dissolved.

Almond Syrup will keep, in an airtight container in the refrigerator, for about 3 days.

meet calvados Calvados is a type of French brandy made from apples in Normandy's Calvados region. If you can't find Calvados, try subbing in applejack, Armagnac, or brandy (though with the latter two you'll be missing out on some of Calvados's mild apple flavor).

topanga
canyon
JULEP

FROM **DAVE KUPCHINSKY, LOS ANGELES**

I f you're a derby-wearing, mint-loving julep drinker—
or even if you don't care for hats but favor light drinks
with fresh flavors—you will appreciate this. It's an anise-
forward, low-proof julep with white vermouth in place
of the traditional bourbon. It's herbal and fresh, and tastes
like a more sophisticated take on the classic.

The recipe calls for Meletti Anisette, an anise-flavored
Italian digestif, but if you can't find that, try adding Pernod
Pastis in its place. **MAKES 1**

Pinch chopped fresh mint leaves

½ teaspoon Herbes de Provence Syrup (recipe follows)

½ ounce Meletti Anisette (see headnote)

½ ounce white verjus (see Note)

2 dashes lemon bitters

2 ounces dry white vermouth, such as Dolin Dry

Mint sprig and lemon twist, for garnish

1 Combine the chopped mint leaves, herbes de Provence syrup, and Meletti Anisette in a mixing glass and muddle together.

2 Fill a julep cup or highball glass with crushed ice. Pour the mint mixture into the glass (do not strain it), add the verjus, lemon bitters, and vermouth, and stir to combine. Garnish with a sprig of fresh mint and lemon twist and serve with a straw.

NOTE: Verjus (aka verjuice) is a crisp, acidic, nonalcoholic juice made from pressing unripened grapes; like wine, it's available in white and red. You can buy it at a liquor store or online.

herbes de provence SYRUP

makes about ½ cup

1 ½ tablespoons herbes de Provence

1 ½ tablespoons chopped fresh sage leaves

1 cup plus 2 tablespoons sugar

1 cup water

COMBINE THE HERBES DE PROVENCE, sage, sugar, and water in a medium-size saucepan over medium heat and cook, stirring, until the sugar dissolves, 4 minutes. Reduce the heat to a simmer and cook, stirring occasionally, until the mixture reduces by half, 15 minutes. Carefully strain the hot syrup into a heatproof jar, discarding the solids. Let cool before using.

Herbes de Provence Syrup will keep, covered and refrigerated, for about 2 weeks.

U.S.S. WONDRICH

FROM **JEFF "BEACHBUM" BERRY** OF **LATITUDE 29, NEW ORLEANS**

J eff "Beachbum" Berry is considered the king of tiki. He's not only an expert on tropical, Polynesian-inspired drinks, but he also operates his own tiki bar in New Orleans, Latitude 29, which became an immediate hit when it debuted in 2014. I love the idea of tropical drinks because they often come in all sorts of exotic tiki cups and are usually playfully garnished with fresh ingredients, but I am often turned off by how sweet they can be. Latitude 29 is the first tiki bar I've visited that actually serves balanced tropical libations that don't kill you with sugar. Jeff based this drink on the Adonis, a pre-Prohibition cocktail built from equal parts sherry and vermouth, with a dash of bitters. His version is on the savory side, with beautifully nutty notes from the amontillado sherry. In fact, this drink doesn't call for any added sugar at all; rather, sweetness comes naturally from the liquors and pineapple juice. **MAKES 1**

- 1½ ounces amontillado sherry
- ¾ ounce fresh pineapple juice (see Pro Tip)
- ¾ ounce Sabra chocolate-orange liqueur
- ¾ ounce sweet red vermouth, preferably Italian
- Dash Angostura bitters
- Pineapple cube or wedge, for garnish

F ill a cocktail shaker halfway with ice cubes. Add the sherry, pineapple juice, Sabra, vermouth, and bitters, and shake to incorporate. Strain into a coupe glass. Garnish with a pineapple cube stuck on a bamboo cocktail pick or place a pineapple wedge on the rim of the glass.

"intermission drinks" At Latitude 29, Jeff calls low-alcohol cocktails "intermission drinks," because they are meant to be "a light refresher between your first and third full-strength cocktail." Jeff developed this particular drink in tandem with bar manager Brad Smith, in honor of cocktail historian Dave Wondrich's first visit to Latitude 29. (Wondrich likes to chase the first boozy cocktail of the evening with a low-alcohol intermission drink.)

If you can't find fresh juice, feel free to sub in store-bought. Or muddle three fresh pineapple cubes with the other ingredients in the shaker before you add the ice.

fresh
THINKING

FROM **ALEX KRATENA**, FORMERLY OF **ARTESIAN AT THE LANGHAM, LONDON**

T he cold brew coffee trend has been sweeping the country over the past few years, and enterprising baristas have discovered that cold coffee plus tonic water (usually reserved for alcoholic cocktails) yields a uniquely refreshing booze-free beverage. Here, Alex Kratena—formerly the head bartender at Artesian at The Langham hotel in London, a spot that has been named the world's best bar for three consecutive years— amps up this trendy drink with a hit of citrus and whiskey. It's worth noting that Artesian is known for its crazy complicated cocktails, but the following recipe is actually very simple. Thanks to the cold brew, this one makes for a great early(ish) morning tipple.

I am a huge fan of cold brew coffee, which is essentially coffee brewed without heat to yield a smooth drink with less acid. You can make your own cold brew easily at home with myriad devices now available (I use an inexpensive Toddy, which you can buy online for around

$30), or you can pick up bottled cold brew at some markets (brands I like are Stumptown and Blue Bottle). **MAKES 1**

∙∙∙

5 ounces tonic water

¼ ounce fresh yuzu or lemon juice (see box)

1 ounce rye whiskey

¾ ounce cold brew coffee (see headnote)

2-inch piece of orange peel

∙∙∙

Fill a 12-ounce tempered glass (Alex uses a Pyrex beaker) halfway with ice cubes and add the tonic, yuzu juice, rye, and cold brew. Stir gently to combine, then squeeze the orange peel over the glass to express the oils (discard the peel).

---

meet yuzu Yuzu is a Japanese citrus fruit that looks like a lemon but has a flavor that's like a cross between a Meyer lemon, a grapefruit, and a satsuma orange. Yuzu fruits are often available at Asian markets, but if you can't find them, you can use bottled yuzu juice, also available at Asian markets and online. To create a similar home blend, mix equal parts fresh lemon (Meyer lemon if you can find it), grapefruit, and orange juices. You can also sub in fresh lemon juice as a shortcut.

classic
MICHELADA

T he michelada just might be my all-time favorite low-alcohol sipper, thanks to its savory nature.
While restaurants and bars serve gussied-up ver-
sions of this classic Mexican libation, the bare-bones
basics call for a Mexican beer, tomato juice, spices (ideally
the blend Tajín Clásico, which is a combo of salt, chiles,
and lime), and a choice of sauces, like Worcestershire,
soy, or even teriyaki—sometimes mixed together, other
times added separately, depending on who is building
the drink. It ends up tasting sort of like a bloody Mary,
but with a more mellow beer base instead of a vodka
spike. Personally, I like extra spice and acid in mine (bring
on the fresh lime juice!), and a pinch of salt mixed into
the cocktail serves to accentuate its flavors for an extra-
bright-tasting drink.

As is the case with most any recipe, the following is really
a set of guidelines—if you like more or less spice, and more
or less acid, feel free to adjust the measurements to suit your
palate. And you'll find an assortment of creative variations
on page 64. **MAKES 1**

Coarse salt (see Note)

2 lime wedges

2 ounces tomato juice (canned, bottled, or fresh)

1 ounce fresh lime juice

½ ounce hot sauce

¼ ounce Worcestershire sauce

½ teaspoon Tajín Clásico

1 bottle (12 ounces) pale lager, such as Corona Extra, chilled

1 Place about ¼ cup salt on a small plate. Rub the rim of a Collins or pint glass (or a 16-ounce Solo cup—no need to get fancy) with one of the lime wedges to moisten it, then dip the rim in the salt to coat.

2 Combine the tomato juice, lime juice, hot sauce, Worcestershire sauce, Tajín, and a pinch of salt in a small bowl and mix.

3 Fill the prepared glass about three-quarters full with ice cubes and add the tomato juice mixture. Top with beer and garnish with the remaining lime wedge.

NOTE: While a coarse salt rim is traditional, Tajín Clásico is another easy and flavorful option.

variations

1 SEASIDE MICHELADA

Combine 2 ounces clam juice + ¼ ounce hot sauce + ¼ ounce Worcestershire sauce + ½ ounce fresh lime juice + ½ teaspoon Tajín. Top with a pale lager. Garnish with a cooked shrimp.

2 MICHELADA NEGRA

Use a dark Mexican beer, such as Negra Modelo, in place of the pale lager.

3 MAKE-DO MICHELADA

Combine ½ ounce hot sauce + ½ ounce fresh lime juice. Top with pale lager; season to taste with salt and pepper or ½ teaspoon Tajín if you have it.

4 THAI MICHELADA

Switch out the hot sauce for 1 teaspoon or more of Sriracha in its place. Garnish with a fresh chile + Thai basil.

5 SALSA MICHELADA

In place of tomato juice, puree 2 tablespoons of salsa; use that as your tomato flavoring.

cynar flip with IPA

FROM **MATT TOCCO** OF **PINEWOOD SOCIAL, NASHVILLE, TN**

I f you are a fan of egg creams, this is the drink for you. But wait, hold on. Even if you're not a creamy drink person, don't let the word *cream* scare you. I usually stay away from egg drinks at bars because oftentimes they're a bit too heavy for me. But this here cocktail is not! Balanced by the bitterness in both the Cynar (an amaro that derives its name from its primary botanical, artichoke, or *cynara scolymus*) and the India pale ale (IPA), the egg adds lightness with a round mouthfeel thanks to the whole yolk. Overall, the effect is sort of caramely creamy without being too heavy, and definitely not at all too sweet. **MAKES 1**

2 ounces Cynar

2 ounces IPA beer, such as Jackalope Leghorn, chilled

1 large egg

¼ ounce Demerara Syrup (page 27)

Grapefruit peel, for garnish

Combine the Cynar, IPA, egg, and demerara syrup in a cocktail shaker without ice, cover, and shake vigorously to break up the egg, about 1 minute. Add ice, cover, and shake again until the mixture is frothy, about 30 seconds. Strain into a stemmed beer glass and garnish with the grapefruit peel.

the DL on IPA You're probably familiar with India pale ales, those brews with a bitter bite thanks to the addition of hops. (Hops are the flower of the hop plant, of which many species exist, each with its own flavor profile.) But beyond bitterness, what you're looking for in an IPA is a freshness—the beer should actually taste freshly brewed, and that freshness also comes from hops. The Brewers Association—the organization that promotes American craft brewing—recognizes three IPA styles (though many subsets exist): American-Style IPA (very fruity and bitter), Session IPA (medium fruit, medium to high bitterness), and Imperial or Double IPA (very fruity, very bitter, and higher in booze). For this cocktail, an American-Style IPA will work best.

panache
INDOCHINE

FROM **ANDREW SALAZAR & MATTHEW LIGHTNER, NAPA, CA**

I can't get enough of this drink. It calls for a grapefruit-flavored India pale ale, and thanks to the brew's bitterness, balanced with the lemon syrup's acidity, the citrus cuts through any of the drink's sweetness, with an underlying tropical blend of lemongrass, ginger, and grapefruit. This is an incredible sipper that's surprisingly simple; I dare you to drink just one.

To prebatch this drink, multiply all ingredients by the number of guests and combine all ingredients except for the beer. Refrigerate the mixture and add the beer just before serving so it doesn't go flat. **MAKES 1**

3 ounces grapefruit IPA, such as Ballast Point Grapefruit Sculpin, chilled

1 ½ ounces Tangy Lemon Syrup (recipe follows)

¾ ounce London dry gin, such as Bombay Sapphire

½ ounce Ginger-Lemongrass Syrup (recipe follows)

Star anise pod and fresh lime leaf, for garnish (optional)

Fill a rocks glass with crushed ice. Add the grapefruit beer, tangy lemon syrup, gin, and ginger-lemongrass syrup and stir to mix. Garnish with the star anise and lime leaf if you wish.

tangy lemon
SYRUP

makes about 2 cups

---

1 cup fresh lemon juice (from about 6 lemons)

½ cup sugar

½ cup distilled white vinegar

PLACE THE LEMON JUICE IN an airtight container and add the sugar and vinegar. Cover and shake well to dissolve the sugar.

Tangy Lemon Syrup will keep, covered and refrigerated, for 3 to 5 days. Shake well before using.

ginger-lemongrass
SYRUP

makes about 1 cup

---

2 tablespoons finely diced fresh lemongrass or
¼ cup finely chopped jarred lemongrass
(see Note)

3 tablespoons peeled and finely diced fresh ginger
(about a 3-inch knob)

6 ounces (¾ cup) hot water

¾ cup sugar

COMBINE THE LEMONGRASS AND GINGER in a large heatproof measuring cup. Add the hot water and steep, 10 minutes. Add the sugar and stir until it dissolves. Strain through a sieve into a heatproof jar with a lid; discard the solids.

Ginger-Lemongrass Syrup will keep, covered and refrigerated, for about 2 weeks.

NOTE: Lemongrass is usually sold fresh at Asian markets and natural foods supermarkets like Whole Foods. To prepare it, cut off the top two-thirds of the stalk and trim the root. Then peel off the dry outer layer(s) of the stalk to reveal the inner shoot. This is the part you'll want to dice.

SO
RADLER

FROM **JASON EISNER** OF **GRACIAS MADRE, LOS ANGELES**

Perhaps one of the most effortless and refreshing cocktails out there, a radler is composed of a blonde lager mixed with equal parts lemonade or citrus-flavored soda. The radler is believed to have originated in Germany during the early twentieth century when a horde of thirsty cyclists showed up at an inn and bar outside Munich owned by a man named Franz Xaver Kugler. As Kugler gave the cyclists beer, he realized his supplies were running low, so he cut the brew with lemon soda, *et voilà* the radler—which translates to "cyclist" in German—was born.

In place of the more traditional lemon, this radler recipe involves a simple grapefruit syrup that's built from fresh grapefruit juice, grapefruit zest, honey, water, and a hint of rosemary. Since you add the grapefruit juice last, it ends up tasting like fresh juice, with sweet notes of honey and a mild herbal undertone thanks to the rosemary. The syrup really only takes 15 (mostly inactive) minutes to make, after which you're left with building one of the easiest cocktails ever: Just pour beer into a glass and add the syrup. **MAKES 1**

1 bottle (375 ml) sour beer, such as Almanac Citra Sour, chilled (see box, page 74)	¾ ounce Grapefruit-Rosemary Syrup (recipe follows) or more to taste

Fill a pint glass three-quarters full with the sour beer (feel free to drink the rest!). Add the grapefruit-rosemary syrup and stir gently to combine. Add ice cubes to fill the glass.

variation

GRAPEFRUIT WINE

When I was testing recipes for this book, I had quite a bit of this Grapefruit-Rosemary Syrup left over. At the time, I was editing an *Eater* article on a popular new trend in France, grapefruit wine (simply rosé wine plus grapefruit juice), and I decided to try it out with this syrup in place of the juice. I mixed 5 ounces of chilled rosé and 1 ounce of this grapefruit syrup in a wineglass with an ice cube and a rosemary sprig garnish. And there you have it, my newest obsession: this light and refreshing grapefruit wine.

PRO TIP If you add too much syrup to your beer and it's a bit too sweet, cut it with a pinch of salt.

WTF is sour beer?! If you've never tried sour beer before, now is the time! True to its name, sour beer is, well, sour, and is known for its funky, acidic, mouth-puckering flavors. While sours are just now gaining widespread popularity, the style isn't as new as you might think. Prior to the advent of refrigeration, almost all beer was sour to a degree, as wild yeast would often invade and colonize beer, imparting a tangy or funky taste. And while those flavors back then were unintentional, these days brewers make beers that highlight these characteristics by brewing with specific bacteria and yeast strains like *Pediococcus*, *Lactobacillus*, and *Brettanomyces*.

Many different types of sour beer exist on the market. Some are brewed with hops, others with fruit and spices. For this recipe, look for a sour beer that's brewed with Citra hops, which impart a citrusy grapefruit note.

grapefruit-rosemary
SYRUP

makes about 1½ cups

¾ cup water

¼ cup honey

3 sprigs fresh rosemary

1 piece (3 inches by 1 inch) grapefruit peel

1½ cups fresh grapefruit juice (from 2 grapefruits),
strained to remove pulp and seeds

---

1 Combine the water, honey, rosemary, and grapefruit peel in a small saucepan over medium-high heat and stir to dissolve the sugar. Bring to a boil, then reduce the heat to medium and simmer, stirring occasionally, until the syrup has reduced by two-thirds, about 15 minutes. Remove from the heat and let cool.

2 Remove and discard the rosemary. Pour the syrup into a glass jar, then add the grapefruit juice. Cover and shake to incorporate.

Grapefruit-Rosemary Syrup will keep, covered and refrigerated, for about 1 week.

hot in the
CITY

FROM **FRANCIS VERRALL** OF **McCARREN HOTEL AND POOL, BROOKLYN, NY**

hen I first moved to Los Angeles in 2006, I used to frequent a nightclub called Hyde. There, I fell for a red pepper–flavored cocktail called the Love Unit. It's the first red-pepper drink I've enjoyed, because I am not hugely keen on the flavor of red peppers in general.

When I tried Hot in the City, it immediately reminded me of the Love Unit in low-ABV form. This festive orange sipper skews savory thanks to the bitter Aperol and grape-fruit juice, in addition to the spice and vegetal notes in the red pepper syrup. The mezcal adds a subtle smoky flavor, while the lime adds brightness. Simply put, this is the per-fect drink for a hot day. **MAKES 1**

½ ounce mezcal

1 ounce Aperol

3 ounces fresh grapefruit
   juice

¾ ounce fresh lime juice

1½ ounces Red Pepper
   Syrup (recipe follows)

Lime wheel, for garnish

1 Combine the mezcal, Aperol, grapefruit juice, lime juice, and red pepper syrup in a cocktail shaker and fill halfway with ice cubes. Cover and shake to chill, 10 seconds.

2 Fill a highball glass three-quarters full with ice cubes. Double-strain the cocktail into it and garnish with the lime wheel.

red pepper SYRUP

makes 2 cups

---

1 cup water

1 cup agave syrup

¼ medium-size red bell pepper,
stemmed and seeded

1-inch piece red chile pepper, such as Holland or
Long Red Chile, stemmed (seeds and pith
removed to reduce heat, if desired)

---

1 Heat the water in a small saucepan over low heat until it simmers, about 3 minutes. Add the agave syrup and remove the pan from the heat. Stir to dissolve the agave syrup, then set aside and let cool to room temperature.

2 Place the agave mixture, red pepper, and chile pepper in a blender and blend on high until the peppers are completely broken down. Strain the mixture through a fine-mesh sieve into a glass jar, cover, and refrigerate.

Red Pepper Syrup will keep, covered and refrigerated, for 1 month.

BUT FIRST, A COCKTAIL

Classic and Creative Aperitifs

Perhaps thanks in part to the recent Spritz revival, preprandial aperitif cocktails are making a comeback. While aperitifs like sherry— cue images of your great-aunt Maude sipping a glass daintily on her brocade couch—can still feel a little bit like a throwback, they are drinks that are slowly being seen in a new light, whether enjoyed neat or mixed into cocktails. But what really unifies these drinks is that they're meant to whet the appetite and not bog you down in heavy, creamy textures and saccharine sweetness. Light on the palate and crisp in flavor, they're liveliness in a glass.

In more civilized parts of the world, like France and Italy, it's still common for people to commence a meal with an aperitif or *aperitivo*. While in France this low-alcohol beverage is often wine based, such as a Kir (white wine plus cassis liqueur) or Kir Royale (the same combo, made with Champagne), Italians build their *aperitivi* based on bitter liqueurs like Campari and Aperol, to create a Spritz. Perhaps you've tried a Campari or Aperol Spritz. These bracing, aromatic drinks, often served in white wine glasses, are composed of soda water, sparkling wine, and one of the aforementioned bitter aperitifs.

Here in the United States we have our own take on the predinner drink: the wine spritzer, perhaps the quintessential low-booze beverage that fell out of vogue in the '90s. Though a wine spritzer was classically built from white wine and carbonated water over ice, these days it's coming back in a whole new array of flavors. No longer is the base limited to white wine—today one will also find red and rosé wine spritzers, often flavored with fresh fruit.

But by no means should these tipples be restricted to premeal quaffing. They're equally delicious with or without food, morning, afternoon, and night. Kick your day-drinking game off right with any of the recipes in this chapter.

champagne
COCKTAIL

Though its precise date of origin is unknown, this classic cocktail dates back to at least the mid-1800s and was originally served with crushed ice and a lemon twist. While many associate bubbles with celebratory events, I believe that Champagne can and should be consumed any day of the week, special occasion or not. I often order a glass of Champagne as an aperitif before dinner, but the great thing about bubbles is that they really pair with just about anything, making sparkling wines especially food friendly. In this case, bubbles are tweaked ever so slightly with citrus, sugar, and bitters, offering a new—but actually old—way to consider Champagne. Also note, while these days "Champagne Cocktail" can refer to any sort of drink based on Champagne, this is a classic not to be confused with modern sparkling wine libations. **MAKES 1**

1 sugar cube

2 dashes Angostura bitters

Champagne or other dry
sparkling white wine,
chilled

Lemon twist, orange slice,
or maraschino cherry
(I love Luxardo brand),
for garnish

Place the sugar cube in a Champagne flute and soak it with the bitters. Fill the flute with sparkling wine and garnish as you like.

variation

Make it your own—try subbing in other types of bitters in place of Angostura.

classic
BELLINI

Did you know that the Bellini was invented during the first half of the twentieth century by Giuseppe Cipriani—founder of the Cipriani restaurant chain—in Venice, Italy? While the drink was initially served at another Venice landmark, Harry's Bar, it's now a menu staple at Cipriani outposts from Miami to Moscow.

The Bellini is a straightforward mix of prosecco and white peach puree, so it's easy to change up with different types of pureed fruit. **MAKES 1**

....

3 ounces prosecco or other dry sparkling white wine, chilled

1 ounce fresh or defrosted frozen white peach puree (see Note)

....

Pour the prosecco into a Champagne flute or white wine glass. Add the peach puree and stir to mix.

NOTE: Peach puree is available at some liquor stores, gourmet food stores, and online, but it's easy (and delicious) to make your own: Puree a peeled, pitted peach in a blender or food processor. If the peach isn't particularly sweet, you can add Simple Syrup (page 26) to taste.

variations

In place of peaches, try subbing in:

- 2 ounces of pureed strawberries or 2 large strawberries muddled into a pulp
- 2 ounces of pureed raspberries or 8 raspberries muddled into a pulp
- 2 ounces of fresh orange juice
- 2 ounces of fresh grapefruit juice
- The seeds and pulp from 1 passion fruit

Kumquat
SANGAREE

FROM **EMPLOYEES ONLY, NEW YORK CITY**

S angaree, the precursor to sangria, is a classic category of cocktails made popular around the mid-1800s. It often consisted of some wine with sugar and nutmeg or other spice. The drink was lost to obscurity during Prohibition and would later be repackaged as sangria at the 1964 World's Fair. This recipe carries on the spirit of the original cocktail with sparkling wine sweetened with candied fruit (instead of sugar) and allspice replacing the nutmeg.

You'll note that the Kumquat Syrup recipe makes more than the ½ ounce needed for the sangaree. In fact, you'll be able to get 6 to 8 drinks out of it—making this an ideal party drink. **MAKES 1**

. . . .

4 ounces prosecco or other dry sparkling white wine, chilled

½ ounce Kumquat Syrup plus 1 tablespoon candied kumquats with several allspice berries (recipe follows)

. . . .

Pour the prosecco into a Champagne flute and add the kumquat syrup and candied kumquats and allspice berries (from the syrup). Stir gently to combine.

....

kumquat SYRUP

makes about ½ cup

¾ cup sugar

½ cup water

½ cup sliced kumquats (about 19 whole kumquats)

Small handful allspice berries

---

1 Combine the sugar and water in a medium-size saucepan over medium-low heat and cook, stirring, until the sugar dissolves, about 3 minutes. Set the syrup aside and let cool.

2 Place ½ cup of the syrup in a jar with a lid, add the kumquats and allspice berries, and cover. Let steep, covered in the refrigerator, overnight.

Kumquat Syrup will keep, covered and refrigerated, for about 1 week.

maman's
orangeless
MIMOSA

FROM **MAMAN, NEW YORK CITY**

When I first tried this cocktail, I was urged to guess its ingredients. To start, it looks exactly like a mimosa, and because of its pale orange hue, my mind kept going to citrus. But it doesn't really taste of citrus, and I couldn't quite place its flavor, which was at once refreshing, mildly vegetal, and a little bit tropical. Turns out the standard orange is replaced with spaghetti squash! The result is an unexpectedly delicious and fun sub for the typical mimosa—try to make your friends guess its ingredients!

This is one of the few drinks in the book for which a juicer is absolutely essential. Sorry to say it, but you just won't get the same results with a blender and cheesecloth. So if you have a juicer, even more reason to try this drink. **MAKES 1**

2 medium-size spaghetti
squash (to yield
1½ ounces fresh juice)

4 ounces Champagne

or other dry sparkling
white wine, chilled

½ ounce banana liqueur

1 Using a vegetable peeler, peel and discard the skin from the squash. Slice the squash in half lengthwise using a chef's knife. Scoop out and discard the seeds and loose, stringy pulp with a sturdy metal spoon. Cut the remaining flesh into 1-inch cubes.

2 Using a juicer, juice the squash cubes.

3 Pour 3 ounces of the Champagne into a Champagne flute. Add the banana liqueur and then the squash juice. Top with the remaining Champagne.

wine SPRITZER

T he cool thing about wine spritzers is that they're like (a) the easiest cocktail ever and (b) a blank slate on which you can make nearly countless ingredient variations. Once you have the foundations of dry white wine and soda water, you can pretty much add whatever fruit juice or syrup you have lying around the house.

I've given you the basic formula—and you can certainly stop there—but adding in fun fruit and herb combinations takes the drink to the next level. I've listed a few of my favorite variations on page 96. You can use a juicer to make them (juicing the ingredients will make a lighter drink, no pulp), but a blender works well, too: Simply combine the ingredients in a blender and turn it on! The fruit-and-wine combinations make enough for one drink— sometimes a bit extra. Simply pour the desired amount of fruit mixture into the glass, then top with soda water.

Also, a note on wine: While I suggest using a dry white, you can also use a sweet wine like Riesling. If you choose to go that route, omit the simple syrup from the fruit mixture. **MAKES 1**

....

3 ounces dry white wine, such as Sauvignon Blanc, chilled

1 ounce soda water

....

Pour the wine into a rocks glass, add an ice cube or two, and top with the soda water. That's it!

variations

1 CANTALOUPE-MINT

Combine 4 ounces dry white wine + 1 ounce
St-Germain + ½ ounce fresh lime juice + 3 cubes
(1 inch each) cantaloupe + 2 fresh mint leaves

2 PASSION FRUIT–SAFFRON

Combine 4 ounces dry white wine + the edible
seeds and flesh of 1 passion fruit (or 1 ounce
passion fruit juice) + ½ ounce Simple Syrup
(page 26) + ¼ ounce fresh lime juice + a pinch
saffron threads

3 MANGO-YUZU

Combine 4 ounces dry white wine + 2 cubes
(2 inches each) mango + ½ ounce Simple Syrup
(page 26) + ½ ounce fresh yuzu or lemon juice

4 GRAPEFRUIT-ROSEMARY

4 ounces dry white wine + 1 ounce Grapefruit-
Rosemary Syrup (page 75)

5 STRAWBERRY-PEACH

4 ounces dry white wine + 2 hulled strawberries
+ ¼ pitted peach + ½ ounce Simple Syrup
(page 26) + ½ ounce fresh lime juice

Kir
ROYALE

T he Kir Royale and its more demure kin, the Kir, are two of the most iconic French cocktails. Fruity and well-balanced—never cloying—the Kir Royale is simplicity itself: a combination of Champagne (or dry white wine, for a Kir) and the Burgundian black currant liqueur, crème de cassis. **MAKES 1**

. . . .

1 ounce crème de cassis

4 ounces Champagne or other dry sparkling white wine, chilled

. . . .

P our the crème de cassis into a Champagne flute and top with the Champagne.

variation

To make a Kir, replace the Champagne with a dry white wine such as Aligote or Chablis, and build the drink in a wineglass.

AMERICANO

One of the most classic of classic cocktails is the Negroni, a bittersweet, orangey tipple built of gin, Campari, and sweet vermouth. The Americano is sort of like the Negroni's laid-back sister. The story behind this legendary libation is that in Florence, Italy, during the early twentieth century, hip cafés offered a drink then known as the "Milano Torino" or the "Mi To," named after the cocktail's two constituents: Campari from Milan and vermouth from Torino. Americans who tried the drink would ask for sparkling water to be added, and hence the Americano was born. This libation would eventually serve as the inspiration behind the Negroni: Add gin, leave out soda water. **MAKES 1**

2 ounces Campari

2 ounces sweet red vermouth

Soda water

Orange slice, for garnish

Fill a wineglass halfway with ice cubes. Add the Campari and vermouth, top with soda water, and stir gently. Garnish with the orange slice.

variations

- Replace the vermouth with 1 ounce Lillet Rosé or ¾ ounce St-Germain or 1 ounce Cocchi Aperitivo Americano.
- Replace the Campari with 1 ounce Aperol or ¾ ounce Cynar or 1 ounce Cardamaro.
- Make a Mi To: Mix equal parts Campari and vermouth and serve over ice.

classic
SPRITZ

I credit New York restaurant Wildair with turning me into a Spritz lover. While I had tried Campari and Aperol Spritzes in the past, it really wasn't until I tried their version that the drink became my new go-to. Traditionally, this highly refreshing, bittersweet drink is made with prosecco, either Aperol (my preference) or Campari, a splash of soda water, and an orange slice. But Wildair actually builds this classic Italian *aperitivo* with a sparkling French white wine instead of the typical prosecco, and they use an Italian Americano (a type of aromatized wine—the word *americano* refers not to the United States but to the root word *amer*, which means bitter) from Italy's Piedmont region. While the following recipe is the classic, make sure to try Wildair's version on page 105. **MAKES 1**

3 to 4 ounces prosecco or other dry sparkling white wine, chilled

2 ounces Aperol or Campari

Splash soda water

Orange slice, for garnish

Pour the prosecco and Aperol into a wineglass or rocks glass with 1 ice cube. Add the soda water and stir gently to combine. Garnish with the orange slice.

Variations

- Although Campari and Aperol are the classic bitter aperitifs mixed into this drink, there's a whole world more out there. Try subbing in your favorite amaro, like Amaro Nonino or Cardamaro, for Aperol or Campari.
- Wildair's Vergano Americano Spritz: Place 3 ice cubes in a wineglass and add 2 ounces of Vergano Americano and enough Les Capriades or other French dry sparkling white wine to fill the glass about three-quarters full (omit the soda water). Stir gently to combine, and add an orange twist.

PRO TIP

Orange is the traditional Spritz garnish, and it's one that I find imperative to incorporate—without it, a Spritz tends to taste a bit flat. Beyond adding visual appeal to the glass, the orange flavor heightens the cocktail's freshness and vibrancy.

port of VENETO

FROM **MARTIN CATE** OF **WHITECHAPEL, SAN FRANCISCO**

S imilar to a Spritz (see page 103), this cocktail calls for a base of prosecco, but for sweeteners it splits the difference between orgeat—an almond syrup—and the amaro. What you end up with is a spicier, more savory aperitif. And while the orange peel acts as a garnish, the oils in the skin will add a kiss of citrus. **MAKES 1**

· ·

½ ounce Amaro di Angostura or Amaro Montenegro (see box)

¼ ounce orgeat (see Note)

4 ounces prosecco or other dry sparkling white wine, chilled

Orange peel (about 2 inches long) and fresh mint leaf, for garnish

· ·

P our the amaro and orgeat into a Champagne flute. Swirl to combine, then top with the prosecco. Twist the orange peel to express its oil on the surface of the drink, then drop it in. Garnish with the mint leaf.

NOTE: In this recipe, Martin suggests going with a store-bought small-batch brand of orgeat, such as Small Hands Foods or Wilks & Wilson, both of which are sold online. But if you'd prefer, you can make your own—it's not too hard. See page 28 for the recipe.

meet amaro di angostura and amaro montenegro

Amaro di Angostura is a recently launched amaro made by the same company behind classic Angostura bitters. Expect spiced notes of cinnamon and clove, plus chocolate and licorice, in this sweet liqueur.

Anyone who works in the bar industry knows that Fernet-Branca, a bitter minty potation, is the unofficial bartenders' handshake. It's *the* go-to bartender shot. But recently bartenders have been putting down the Fernet and instead reaching for Amaro Montenegro—a nineteenth-century drink conceived in Bologna, Italy, that's composed of forty botanicals including orange peel and coriander.

law-abiding
CITIZEN

FROM **RYAN GANNON** OF **CURE, NEW ORLEANS**

T his cocktail is just stellar! The nutty notes of the amontillado sherry harmonize beautifully with the pomegranate liqueur, and the lemon juice contributes the acidity that one would find in a fresh pomegranate. **MAKES 1**

∙∙

¾ ounce pomegranate liqueur, such as PAMA

1½ ounces amontillado sherry, such as Hidalgo Napoleon

¾ ounce fresh lemon juice

¼ ounce Simple Syrup (page 26)

Bittermens 'Elemakule Tiki Bitters, for garnish (optional, but recommended)

∙∙

C ombine the pomegranate liqueur, sherry, lemon juice, and simple syrup in a cocktail shaker. Add ice cubes to fill three-quarters full. Cover and shake until the shaker is frosty, about 15 seconds. Double-strain into a coupe glass. Top with four drops of the bitters, if you like.

django
REINHARDT

FROM **ERICK CASTRO** OF **POLITE PROVISIONS, SAN DIEGO**

V ermouth might be best known for its role in the martini, but there's so much more to the aromatized wine. While awesome new domestic producers are beginning to pop up—like Uncouth Vermouth from Brooklyn, New York, and Portland, Oregon's Hammer & Tongs—bartenders are getting even more creative, using vermouth as the main component of a drink, as opposed to using it more like a seasoning. Consider wine- and fruit-based cocktails like the Rosé All Day on page 45 or the Grapefruit Wine on page 73: You can use vermouth in the same way, mixing the wine with fruit, as Erick Castro did in this recipe. I suggest this in place of your usual mimosa. **MAKES 1**

| 3 ounces dry white vermouth | ¾ ounce Simple Syrup (page 26) |
| ¾ ounce fresh lemon juice | 3 orange slices |

1 Combine the vermouth, lemon juice, simple syrup, and 2 of the orange slices in a cocktail shaker and muddle to break down the orange. Add ice cubes to fill the shaker three-quarters full, cover, and shake to chill, about 15 seconds.

2 Fill a rocks glass with ice cubes and strain the cocktail over the ice. Garnish with the remaining orange slice.

dolores
PARK

FROM **CAITLIN LAMAN** OF **TRICK DOG, SAN FRANCISCO**

U nless you live in the UK, where sloe berries grow plentifully, it's highly possible you've never heard of sloe gin—a gin-based liquor infused with small, blue, intensely flavorful berries that look and taste a bit like blueberries. For this libation, sloe berries impart the flavor of blueberries, and there's something about the briny, mildly nutty nature of Manzanilla sherry that perfectly complements the hit of absinthe. Overall, this balanced cocktail slants slightly herbaceous, with a berry undertone. **MAKES 1**

1 ounce Manzanilla sherry, such as La Cigarrera

¼ ounce sloe gin, such as Sipsmith

½ ounce fresh lemon juice

¼ ounce Rich Simple Syrup (page 26)

4 dashes absinthe, such as Vieux Pontarlier

6 fresh raspberries

Lemon wheel, for garnish

1 Place the sherry, sloe gin, lemon juice, rich simple syrup, absinthe, and 3 of the raspberries in a cocktail shaker. Add ice cubes to fill three-quarters full, cover, and shake to chill, about 15 seconds.

2 Fill an old-fashioned glass with crushed ice. Strain the cocktail into the glass and garnish with the remaining raspberries and the lemon wheel.

FÊTE POIRE

FROM **GILLIAN HELQUIST,** FORMERLY OF **SHED, NAPA, CA**

This cocktail tastes like vanilla cake—in the best possible way. The pear syrup is incredible on its own, and it's not too sweet thanks to the healthy cup of dry white wine that's mixed in. After you make the syrup (which can be prepared ahead), you'll have a bunch of leftover pear quarters. Don't throw them away—they're delicious! Try serving them at room temperature or slightly warm, with a scoop of vanilla ice cream. **MAKES 1**

½ ounce Pear Syrup (recipe follows)

½ ounce Orgeat Syrup (page 28)

1 teaspoon fresh lemon juice

2 ounces dry white vermouth

2 dashes cardamom bitters, such as Scrappy's

Paper-thin pear slices, for garnish (optional)

Combine the pear syrup, orgeat syrup, lemon juice, vermouth, and bitters in a cocktail shaker. Add ice cubes to fill three-quarters full, cover, and shake until chilled, about 15 seconds. Strain into a coupe glass and float a couple of pear slices on top, if you like.

pear SYRUP

makes about 1¾ cups

---

2 green pears, preferably D'Anjou,
peeled, cored, and quartered

1 cup dry white wine

½ cup water

½ cup sugar

1 bay leaf

¼-inch piece vanilla bean

½ teaspoon salt

---

1 Combine the pears, wine, water, sugar, bay leaf, vanilla bean, and salt in a heavy-bottomed saucepan over medium-high heat. Bring to a gentle simmer, then cover with parchment paper and cook, undisturbed, until the pears are tender, about 20 minutes. Remove from the heat and let cool.

2 Use a slotted spoon to remove the pears from the liquid (reserve them for another use), and carefully pour the syrup into a glass jar or bottle.

Pear Syrup will keep, covered and refrigerated, for 1 week.

WARM ME UP
Spiked Coffees, Toddies, and Other Hot Drinks

Every holiday season, I can't help but get excited about preparing mulled wine. There's something about the comfort of gripping a hot mug perfumed with orange and spice that draws me in. But wine isn't the only player in spiked hot drinks. How about tea and coffee, and even hot chocolate?!

While it's obviously much more common to find cold cocktails, hot boozy drinks can be just as tasty, especially on a cold afternoon. And with a hot beverage, you don't need as much liquor for that warming feeling. While Irish coffee has been long established as a drink that will give you pep in more than one way (and you'll find some surprising variations on page 124), with the explosion of craft coffee, bartenders have taken to mixing hot drinks with excellent third-wave roasts. The same goes for tea. Tea-based tipples are traditionally mixed with whiskey, but I am especially keen on the addition of darker sherries. The nutty, roasty, umami-esque flavors of these fortified wines almost taste naturally warm, and serve as a prime addition to hot drinks that are also low-ABV.

irish
COFFEE

Sometimes you need an extra morning pick-me-up—call it hair of the dog or simply a great way to start your day. Recently, I've become a supporter of boozy coffee drinks, be it night or day, because sometimes you need that caffeine kick. Since Irish coffee calls for the same ingredients some might add to their morning brew—brown sugar and cream, with the addition of booze—this simple recipe is like a blank slate for customization. Try changing up the dairy (or opt for a non-dairy alternative), choosing a different sweetener, adding a dollop of freshly whipped cream (see page 123), or even throwing in some spices (see page 124 for a bunch of variations). But remember, for a true Irish coffee, don't skip the booze! **MAKES 1**

....

5 ounces freshly brewed
   hot coffee

1 tablespoon brown sugar

1½ ounces heavy
   (whipping) cream

1 ounce whiskey

....

Pour the coffee, brown sugar, cream, and whiskey into a mug and stir to combine.

....

homemade
WHIPPED CREAM

makes 2½ cups

---

1 cup heavy (whipping) cream

1 tablespoon sugar (or more to taste)

2 teaspoons pure vanilla extract (optional)

COMBINE THE CREAM, SUGAR, AND vanilla in a medium-size bowl and whip with an electric mixer at high speed until stiff peaks form, about 3 minutes.

Homemade Whipped Cream will keep, in an airtight container in the refrigerator, for 4 hours.

variations

1 DIRTY CHAI

Dirty chai is chai plus coffee and it's delicious. Set a pour-over dripper on a mug, fill it with 2 tablespoons ground coffee, and pour 6 ounces brewed chai tea over the coffee. Proceed with the recipe as directed.

2 GO TROPICAL

In place of the heavy cream, use 1½ ounces coconut milk and 1 teaspoon coconut butter.

3 NUTTY MOCHA

In place of the heavy cream, use 2 ounces hazelnut milk and 1 tablespoon unsweetened cocoa powder.

4 CHILL OUT

This one is inspired by Vietnamese iced coffee. Brew your coffee double strength. Fill a cocktail shaker three-quarters full of ice cubes, carefully add the hot coffee, and add 1 tablespoon sweetened condensed milk along with the sugar and whiskey (omit the heavy cream). Cover and shake vigorously to blend and chill, 15 seconds.

CUSK

FROM **RYAN CHETIYAWARDANA** OF **WHITE LYAN, LONDON**

O ften coffee cocktails incorporate some form of dairy, making them a bit heavy. But what's so brilliant about this recipe is that Ryan Chetiyawardana, a bartender known for his boundary-pushing, molecular drinks, actually replaces any milk with a brown butter syrup; when you sip this drink, it's super light with just a touch of extra body. You'll also taste the bready caraway notes from the aquavit. **MAKES 1**

· ·

1 piece (¼ inch thick) fresh, peeled ginger

½ ounce Brown Butter Syrup (recipe follows)

1 ounce aquavit (see box, page 128)

½ cup freshly brewed hot coffee

1 dash grapefruit bitters, such as Fee Brothers

Lemon twist, for garnish

· ·

P lace the ginger in a mug and add the butter syrup and aquavit. Stir in the coffee and bitters. Garnish with a lemon twist.

brown butter
SYRUP

makes 1½ cups

½ cup (1 stick) unsalted butter

Pinch salt

2 cups plus 4 tablespoons demerara sugar

1¼ cups water

1 Combine the butter and salt in a medium-size saucepan over medium heat and cook, swirling the butter in the pan. The butter will melt and then begin to foam and crackle. Cook, stirring constantly with a heatproof silicone spatula, until the butter solids—the little specks at the bottom of the pan—turn golden brown and smell nutty and toasty, about 3 minutes (watch it carefully as it cooks; it burns easily!).

2 Working quickly and carefully, stir in the sugar and water and, stirring constantly, bring the mixture to a boil. Immediately remove it from the heat and transfer the syrup to a heatproof bowl. Refrigerate the syrup until it separates and the fat rises to the top, about 3 hours.

3 Using a spoon, skim and discard the fat from the top of the syrup. Strain the syrup through a fine-mesh sieve into a glass jar, cover, and refrigerate until ready to use.

Brown Butter Syrup will keep, covered in the refrigerator, for about 1 week.

meet aquavit Although aquavit is ubiquitous in Scandinavia, the liquor's popularity has grown here in the United States in the last couple of years. Distilled from grain, aquavit's main flavor is caraway—giving it a uniquely savory, bready flavor—and distillers add other complementary botanicals to create their spirit's proprietary recipe. While the Danes and Swedes down shots of aquavit when among friends, Norwegians sip the spirit with dinner. Here in the United States, aquavit is beginning to appear in cocktails, and mixing the liquor (which is 42 to 45 percent ABV) with other liquids helps it pack a gentler punch.

Jerez TODDY

FROM **ALBA HUERTA** OF **JULEP, HOUSTON, TX**

J erez de la Frontera, in Andalusia, Spain, is sherry's ancestral home, where numerous styles of the oxidative, fortified wine are produced in flavors from saline to sweet. This spiced toddy features two types—a mixture of sweet Pedro Ximénez sherry blended with a splash of dry Palo Cortado sherry. Together the wines have a deep, raisiny flavor that complements the cinnamon tea.

Because the cinnamon tea recipe used here yields 32 ounces, you can batch up this cocktail to suit 10 by multiplying the rest of the ingredients by 10. In that case, just add them directly to the pot you used to make the tea, then ladle into teacups. **MAKES 1**

3 ounces Cinnamon Tea (recipe follows)

1 ½ ounces Pedro Ximénez sherry

½ ounce Palo Cortado sherry

1 dash Bar Keep Baked Apple Bitters (see Note)

1 cinnamon stick, for garnish

Combine the tea, sherries, and bitters in a teacup and stir gently. Garnish with a cinnamon stick.

NOTE: Think about the flavor of an autumn apple pie—that's what you'll find in Bar Keep Baked Apple Bitters. These bitters are sold at some specialty liquor stores, and from a variety of retailers online.

cinnamon TEA

makes 4 cups

---

1 cinnamon stick

4 cups water

COMBINE THE CINNAMON STICK AND water in a medium-size pot over high heat and bring to a boil. Remove from the heat and let steep, uncovered, about 10 minutes. Return the pot to the heat and bring to a boil a second time. Remove the tea from the heat and remove the cinnamon stick. Let the tea cool slightly before using.

Cinnamon Tea is best used right away.

PRO TIPS

- To turn this cocktail into a nightcap, add a splash of milk.

- The cinnamon stick used for the tea can be brewed several times, so don't discard it after the first use. Let it dry, then store it in a plastic bag or jar for the next time.

chi-chaw
TODDY

FROM **SHAWN CHEN** OF **REDFARM, NEW YORK CITY**

Shawn Chen, the bar honcho at Manhattan's wildly popular modern Chinese restaurant RedFarm, drew inspiration for this hot tipple from traditional Chinese tea ceremonies. Specifically, he chose osmanthus oolong tea—a type of oolong that's mixed with buttery osmanthus flowers—for its delicate aroma. The tea's nutty taste serves as a backdrop to support the warm flavors of whiskey and honey, plus the zip of ginger and lemon. The toddy incorporates traditional cold-fighting ingredients, making it the perfect mild intoxicant for those feeling a bit under the weather. Also note: Because the tea recipe makes enough for about three drinks, if you're looking to batch this one, just multiply each of the other ingredients by three. **MAKES 1**

¾ ounce rye whiskey (Shawn likes George Dickel Rye)

¼ ounce Benedictine (see box)

½ ounce Sugared Ginger (recipe follows)

½ ounce fresh lemon juice

¼ ounce honey

2½ ounces hot brewed osmanthus oolong tea (recipe follows)

Fresh mint leaf and lemon wheel studded with cloves, for garnish

Combine the whiskey, Benedictine, sugared ginger, lemon juice, honey, and oolong tea in a teacup. Stir to blend. Garnish with the mint leaf and clove-studded lemon wheel.

meet benedictine Benedictine is a syrupy sweet herbal liqueur developed in France during the nineteenth century. Though some people prefer to sip it neat, it's a popular ingredient in cocktails, where it contributes sweetness and body, in addition to a complex backbone of subtly spiced flavors. While Benedictine's recipe is secret, we do know that the liqueur starts with a cognac base and includes botanicals like saffron, cinnamon, and juniper.

sugared GINGER

makes 1 cup

½ cup coarsely chopped peeled fresh ginger
(about eight ½-inch pieces)

1 cup superfine sugar

PUREE THE GINGER IN A blender. Transfer it to an air-tight container, add the sugar, and stir until it dissolves.

Sugared Ginger will keep, covered in the refrigerator, for up to 2 weeks.

. . . .

osmanthus OOLONG TEA

makes 1 cup

---

2 teaspoons loose osmanthus oolong tea

8 ounces boiling water

PLACE THE LOOSE TEA IN a tea strainer and set inside a teacup. Add the boiling water and let steep, 3 to 5 minutes. Discard the tea leaves and use hot.

GLÜHWEIN

FROM **CRAIG LANE** OF **BAR AGRICOLE, SAN FRANCISCO**

D uring the winter, and especially when organizing holiday gatherings, mulled wine is my
go-to. Not only is hot spiced wine incredibly
simple to make—you're basically dumping a
bunch of ingredients into a pot and cooking—but the out-
come of the drink always tastes far more complex than the
effort that went into making it. Sometimes mulled wine
can be a bit too sweet: The heat of the drink masks the
sugar, but if you don't finish your mug right away and the
wine cools down a bit, suddenly the sweetness can wallop
you. Happily, this recipe is the exception. Not too sweet,
but just sweet enough, it tastes like the holidays in a glass.
Note that it makes enough for a big party, but you can
easily scale it down by cutting the recipe in half or even a
quarter. **MAKES ABOUT 40**

8 bottles (750 ml each) dry, fruity red wine, such as Pinot Noir or Beaujolais

1¼ cups sugar

8 cinnamon sticks

3 oranges studded with cloves, then sliced into ½-inch-thick wheels

30 whole cloves

¼ teaspoon ground mace

¼ teaspoon ground allspice

¼ teaspoon ground nutmeg

Peel of 2 lemons

2½ cups brandy, such as Armagnac or Cognac

1 bottle (750 ml) kirsch or maraschino liqueur, for serving

1 Combine the wine, sugar, cinnamon sticks, clove-studded orange wheels, cloves, mace, allspice, nutmeg, and lemon peel in a 9-quart stockpot over low heat. Cook, stirring occasionally, until the sugar dissolves and the mixture begins to simmer, 15 minutes.

2 Add the brandy and simmer, stirring occasionally, for another 15 minutes. Do not allow the mixture to boil.

3 Strain the mixture through a fine-mesh sieve set over a large heatproof bowl, pressing the oranges with the back of a spoon to extract the juice; discard the solids. Return the Glühwein to the pot and keep warm, over low heat. To serve, pour ½ ounce of the kirsch into each mug and top with ½ cup of the Glühwein.

the warm
EMBRACE

FROM **LUCINDA STERLING** OF **MIDDLE BRANCH, NEW YORK CITY**

I magine the flavor of autumn captured in a mug. Apple and cinnamon, plus warm, woody notes from the whiskey. Serve it warm or, during the summer, let the drink cool then pour it over crushed ice. **MAKES 1**

2 ounces hot brewed apple cinnamon tea, such as Celestial Seasonings

1 ounce whiskey (such as Stranahan's)

1 ounce ginger liqueur, such as Domaine de Canton

1 ounce apple cider, warm or at room temperature

½ ounce fresh lemon juice

Ground cinnamon, for garnish

C ombine the tea, whiskey, ginger liqueur, apple cider, and lemon juice in a mug, and stir to mix. Garnish with a sprinkle of ground cinnamon.

chaud
MAMAN

FROM **HUGO SIMBILLIE** OF **MAMAN, NEW YORK CITY**

F or this recipe, feel free to make your favorite form of hot cocoa, whether it's Carnation Instant or a fancier homemade version. Hot cocoa made with water or milk both work, but I'd suggest going with a water base because the amaro and walnut liqueur add body and richness of their own. I was a bit surprised to see sherry in this recipe, but the saline notes of the wine serve to balance out any sweetness in the drink. It also adds a unique savory note, which I love. **MAKES 1**

....

1 ounce fino sherry

1 ounce amaro,
   such as Cardamaro

⅓ ounce walnut liqueur

6 ounces Homemade
   Hot Chocolate
   (recipe follows) or
   prepared hot cocoa of
   your choice

Large marshmallow,
   for garnish

....

C ombine the sherry, amaro, walnut liqueur, and hot chocolate in a cocktail shaker. Cover and shake carefully, with a dishtowel wrapped around the shaker if necessary, to combine. Pour into a mug and top with the marshmallow for garnish.

···

homemade
HOT CHOCOLATE

makes 1 cup

---

1 cup water

2 tablespoons unsweetened cocoa powder

1 teaspoon sugar

Pinch salt

COMBINE THE WATER, COCOA POWDER, sugar, and salt in a small saucepan over medium heat and cook, whisking occasionally, until the sugar dissolves, about 3 minutes. Continue cooking, whisking occasionally, until the mixture is hot and blended, about 5 minutes.

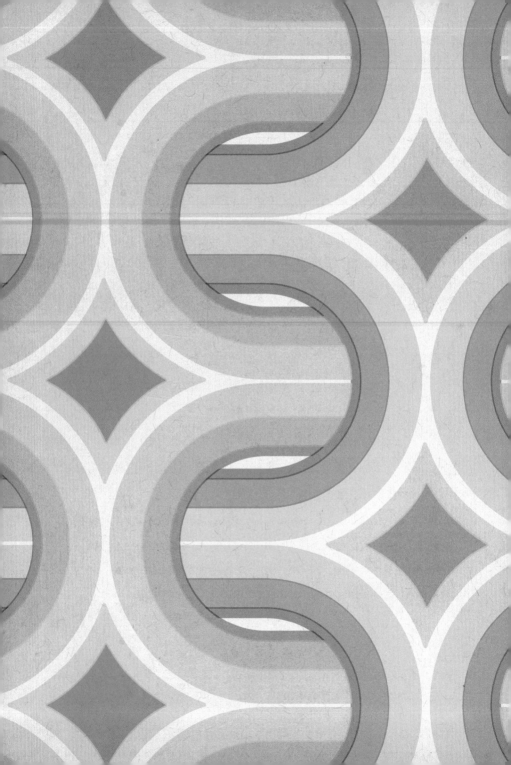

GROUPLOVE
Party-Friendly Potations

I love entertaining. Dinner parties, July Fourth barbecues, birthdays—you name it and I've thrown a party for it. But the biggest challenge with entertaining is wanting to serve guests the best possible food and drink without being tied to the kitchen the whole time. So, when planning parties, I always look to food and drink that can be premade, or at least partly prepped in advance. Luckily, cocktails are especially conducive to prebatching (see page 152 for tips on how to do this)! The idea being that you can make some drinks hours, or even days, in advance, and then just serve them once your guests arrive.

I am a huge fan of punches like mulled wine in the winter and sangria in the summer. But festive, large-format drinks extend beyond these mainstays. Up next, creative communal cocktails flavored with mint tea, rose water, ginger, and more!

friends with BENEFITS

FROM **GABE ORTA & ELAD ZVI** OF **THE BROKEN SHAKER, MIAMI**

Rosé is one of those wines that just go down so easily, especially on a hot day with friends. So why not use rosé as a base for punch? That's exactly what The Broken Shaker guys have done with this number. Think mildly boozy, bubbly adult lemonade with a soft ginger undertone. Since this is a punch, you can use an ice ring or Bundt pan to freeze a large block of ice; otherwise standard cubes work, too (I like to freeze edible flowers in the ice—see page 30 for instructions). Whatever you choose, good luck drinking just one glass! **SERVES 4 TO 6**

4 cups ginger beer, such as Fever-Tree

2 cups fresh lemon juice

1 bottle (750 ml) rosé wine, chilled

1 bottle (750 ml) Cocchi Aperitivo Americano (see box)

10 dashes grapefruit bitters

Lemon wheels, for garnish

Assorted edible flowers (see headnote), for garnish (optional)

P lace an ice ring or 3 cups ice cubes in a punch bowl. Add the ginger beer, lemon juice, rosé, Cocchi Aperitivo Americano, and grapefruit bitters, and stir together gently. Garnish with the lemon wheels and edible flowers, if using. Serve in rocks glasses.

meet cocchi aperitivo americano
As its name suggests, Cocchi Aperitivo Americano is a bittersweet Italian aperitif wine. It was first produced in the late nineteenth century and is made from a base of Moscato d'Asti wine that's been fortified with brandy and flavored with bitter cinchona bark, citrus, and spices (it is 16.5 percent ABV). Cocchi Aperitivo Americano is sort of like the Italian version of Lillet Blanc (see page 38), and can be subbed in recipes that call for that wine. But Cocchi is also great on its own, served over ice with a splash of club soda and an orange slice.

classic
red
SANGRIA

I happily drink sangria—which is essentially a Spanish beverage of sweetened wine with fruit—any time of the year. And the beauty of this libation lies in its versatility. Sangria can be made from red wine, white wine, sparkling wine, or rosé, and an endless array of fruits can be added based on your personal preference, whatever's in season, or what you have at home. Another great thing about sangria is that you can make it without strictly following a recipe. Just start with a wine base, add the fruit juice(s) and chopped fruit of your choice, maybe some spices, and a sweetener if you so desire. **MAKES ABOUT 8**

1 bottle (750 ml) medium-
   bodied dry red wine,
   such as Grenache

1 Granny Smith apple,
   cored and chopped into
   ¾-inch cubes

1 orange, sliced into
   ½-inch-thick half-moons

1 cup fresh orange juice,
   or more to taste

3 tablespoons sugar
   (optional)

1 Combine the wine, apple, orange, orange juice, and
   sugar, if using, in a pitcher, and stir gently. Cover
and refrigerate to let flavors develop, at least 4 hours or
overnight.

2 Fill wineglasses with ice cubes, add the sangria,
   and serve.

how to batch cocktails

The general rule of thumb for batching single-serving cocktails is to multiply each ingredient by the number of drinks you'd like to make. But! You also need to account for ice dilution—a vital component of any cocktail. The easiest way to do this is to make one cocktail without ice and, using a scale, weigh the drink. Then add the ice and shake or stir until chilled, strain out the ice, and weigh the drink again. Subtract the first measurement from the second; the difference equals the amount of water dilution required for a single drink. Next, multiply the water dilution amount by the desired number of drinks—this is how much water you'll need to add to the scaled-up booze mixture.

Here's an example: Let's say a drink weighs 5 ounces without ice and 6 ounces once diluted. The difference (aka amount of water dilution) = 1 ounce. If you want to scale it up to 10 servings: 1 ounce water dilution x 10 (servings) = 10 ounces total water dilution.

Now simply add the amount of total water dilution (10 ounces) to the batched cocktail. Keep the mixture in the fridge until ready to serve—no ice needed!

Other Tips for Scaling Up:

- The best types of cocktails to scale up are those that call for flavored syrups, tea, or other ingredients that won't separate (avoid eggs and dairy). Stay away from drinks that require muddling—it's too much work.

- Bubbly ingredients should always be added just before serving so the drink doesn't go flat.

- If a recipe calls for citrus juice, squeeze it the day of the event so that its flavor remains fresh and bright.

alphabet
city
white
SANGRIA

Years ago, there was a restaurant in New York's Alphabet City that served the most intoxicatingly delicious peach and cantaloupe white sangria. Actually, it was this sangria that got me hooked on the classic red's white twin. During the summer, I used to sit in the restaurant—with its windows wide open, which allowed the summer's lazy heat to seize the space—and sip the cool, crisp, just barely sweet sangria. From my memory, I've re-created the following recipe. **MAKES ABOUT 8**

1 bottle (750 ml) dry,
floral white wine, such
as Muscat (see Note)

1 ½ cups cubed cantaloupe
or other firm melon

1 peach, stemmed, pitted,
and cut into ½-inch
cubes

¾ cup fresh grapefruit juice

2 tablespoons sugar

1 Combine the wine, cantaloupe, peach, grapefruit juice, and sugar in a pitcher, and stir gently. Cover and refrigerate to let the flavors develop, at least 4 hours or overnight.

2 Fill wineglasses with ice cubes, add the sangria, and serve.

NOTE: Because you will be adding other flavors to the wine, choosing a less expensive bottle is A-OK. This is not the time to splurge.

the
regents
ROYALE

FROM **JANE DANGER** OF **MOTHER OF PEARL, NEW YORK CITY**

R emember strawberry-flavored Starburst candy? This tiki-inspired tropical libation literally tastes like the beloved childhood treat. While this delightful drink calls for bubbles, which lower its ABV, it's delicious straight out of the blender, served over ice. But if you want to lower the booze content even more, feel free to leave out the rum.

"Regent's Punch" is a classic recipe (the base for this drink is modeled after it); to "Royale" a cocktail is to top it with sparkling wine (just like the Kir Royale on page 100). The recipe calls for dry curaçao, which is an orange liqueur flavored with the peels of bitter Seville oranges. Combined with the tropical, fruity, and slightly grassy-tasting cachaça (thanks to the green tea infusion) and the drink's other ingredients, the orange flavor enhances the libation's overall exotic strawberry flavor. **SERVES 3**

8 large strawberries, 5 hulled, 3 with greens intact

2¼ ounces fresh lime juice

2¼ ounces pineapple juice, preferably fresh

2¼ ounces Rich Simple Syrup (page 26)

1½ ounces amber-colored rum, such as Smith & Cross

1½ ounces orange liqueur (such as Pierre Ferrand Dry Curaçao)

1½ ounces Green Tea–Infused Cachaça (recipe follows)

1 bottle (375 ml) prosecco or other dry sparkling white wine, chilled

Pineapple cup (optional; see page 158), for serving

Pineapple triangles, lime wheels and leaves, for garnish

1 Combine the 5 hulled strawberries with the lime juice, pineapple juice, rich simple syrup, rum, orange liqueur, and green tea–infused cachaça in a blender and puree.

2 Fill a pineapple cup, if using, or a large (14-ounce) tiki glass with crushed ice. Strain the puree into the glass through a fine-mesh sieve, and insert the bottle of sparkling wine upside down into the drink. (You can leave it in place or remove it once it's emptied out—your choice.)

3 Garnish with the remaining strawberries and the pineapple triangles, lime wheels, and leaves.

make your own pineapple cup

Lay a pineapple on its side and use a chef's knife to slice off the top 1½ inches. (You can reserve some of the pineapple leaves to use as a cocktail garnish.)

Next, use a pineapple corer to remove the flesh from the shell. It will leave behind a center column of tough fruit; remove this inedible piece with the tip of your chef's knife. Alternatively, run a chef's knife between the shell and the flesh of the pineapple, leaving about ½ inch of flesh around the perimeter and making sure not to pierce the bottom of the fruit. Carefully slice the flesh into 4 quarters, then use a spoon to scoop them out.

Fill the pineapple with the desired cocktail and enjoy!

green tea–infused
CACHAÇA

makes 750 ml

2 ounces dried green tea leaves

1 bottle (750 ml) cachaça (see box)

ADD THE GREEN TEA LEAVES to the bottle of cachaça and let infuse at room temperature, 20 minutes. Pour the mixture through a fine-mesh sieve and into a jar.

Green Tea–Infused Cachaça will keep, covered at room temperature, for 2 years.

meet cachaça Some think of cachaça as Brazilian rum. The main difference between cachaça and rum is that cachaça is distilled from fresh sugarcane juice, whereas rum is distilled from molasses (boiled sugarcane juice). A great cachaça is nuanced and tastes like fresh, exotic fruit (I personally prefer unaged cachaça, but many love aged cachaças that take on the flavor of native Brazilian woods, in which they're often aged). I detect a banana-esque sweetness in the liquor, which jibes beautifully with the lime in Brazil's signature drink, the caipirinha.

break the
BANK

FROM **BRIAN MEANS** FORMERLY OF **DIRTY HABIT, SAN FRANCISCO**

lightly reminiscent of a minty julep though with a spicy ginger kick, this cocktail calls for Palo Cortado sherry, and the fortified wine's nutty notes give this drink a sophisticated, complex backbone. Perfect for that Derby Day party, or really any party regardless of the season. If you don't have bourbon at home, feel free to sub in another whiskey. **MAKES 8 TO 10**

. . . .

1 cup Palo Cortado sherry (such as Lustau Almacenista), chilled

½ cup bourbon (such as Larceny), chilled

1 cup brewed mint tea, chilled

5 ounces Ginger Syrup (recipe follows)

5 ounces fresh lemon juice

1 cup prosecco or other dry sparkling white wine, chilled

10 lemon wheels, 10 sprigs fresh mint, and ½ cup raspberries, for garnish

. . . .

Place an ice block or ring in a punch bowl (or 2 cups of ice cubes). Pour in the sherry, bourbon, mint tea, ginger syrup, lemon juice, and prosecco, and stir gently to combine. Decorate the punch with the garnishes.

ginger SYRUP
makes about 2 cups

3 ounces chopped peeled fresh ginger

3 ounces ginger juice (see Note)

1 ¼ cups sugar

1 ¼ cups water

Combine the chopped ginger, ginger juice, sugar, and water in a medium-size saucepan over medium heat. Bring to a boil, then remove from the heat and let steep, 30 minutes. Strain through a fine-mesh sieve set over an airtight container, discarding the solids.

Ginger Syrup will keep, covered and refrigerated, for 1 week.

NOTE: Bottled ginger juice is available at most natural foods super-markets and online, and possibly at your local juice bar.

spring
has
SPRUNG

FROM **MO HODGES** OF **BENJAMIN COOPER, SAN FRANCISCO**

The theme for this cocktail is definitely green—Green Chartreuse, lime juice, plus an abundance of green produce. Hello, spring! Despite all the veg in this cocktail, you actually don't need a juicer to make it. Instead, pile your veggies in a blender and puree them until the mixture takes on a slushy, salsa-like consistency. Then, you can either strain the mixture through a sieve or, even easier, pour it through cheesecloth and squeeze to extract all the green gold. I like to save the leftover pulp and incorporate it into muffins.

You'll see that the recipe calls for ascorbic acid, which despite its unusual-sounding name, is actually just vitamin C. While it's perfectly fine to omit it, its function here is to stabilize color and prevent oxidation. You can find powdered ascorbic acid (aka vitamin C powder) at health food stores and online. **SERVES ABOUT 25**

4 English cucumbers

4 green apples

1 fennel bulb (stalks and fronds discarded)

1 bunch fresh parsley

½ bunch celery, stalks halved

1 tablespoon ascorbic acid (optional)

4 cups London dry gin

3 cups dry vermouth, such as Dolin Blanc

1½ cups Green Chartreuse

1½ cups fresh lime juice

6¾ ounces Simple Syrup (page 26)

1½ cups club soda

1 Cut 3 cucumbers, 3 apples, and the fennel bulb into quarters, and place them in a high-powered blender, along with the parsley, celery, and the ascorbic acid, if using. Puree, pausing occasionally to scrape down the sides of the blender, until the mixture has a soupy, salsa-like consistency.

2 Fill a punch bowl with 3 cups ice cubes. Strain the puree through a fine-mesh sieve or cheesecloth into the bowl (set the pulp aside for another use). Add in the gin, vermouth, Green Chartreuse, lime juice, and simple syrup, and stir gently to combine.

3 Cut the remaining cucumber and apple into ¼-inch-thick slices and float atop the punch. Top with the club soda.

rosa de OAXACA

FROM **JUAN CORONADO** OF **MINIBAR, WASHINGTON, D.C.**

Mezcal and the more common tequila are distilled from different species of the same plant: agave. As part of mezcal's distillation process, the hearts of agave plants—known as *piñas*—are smoked in underground pits for days, a process that ultimately yields an earthy, smoky-tasting spirit in comparison to tequila's clean, vegetal flavor. When mezcal mingles with cucumber, lime, and rose water, as in this punch, the ultimate smoked spa drink is born. As for this drink's name, most mezcal is distilled in Oaxaca, a vibrant state in southern Mexico. **SERVES 7**

1 cup mezcal (see box)

½ cup fresh lime juice

¾ cup Honey Syrup (page 27)

¼ cup cucumber juice (see Notes)

¾ ounce food-grade rose water (see Notes)

¼ cup prosecco or other dry sparkling white wine, chilled

Organic rose petals, preferably white, and cucumber coins, for garnish

Place the mezcal, lime juice, honey syrup, cucumber juice, and rose water in a punch bowl, and stir to combine. Add a block of ice and set aside to chill, 7 minutes. Add the sparkling wine and garnish with the rose petals and cucumber coins.

NOTES: You can use a juicer to make fresh cucumber juice, or a local juice bar can easily press it, too. If you don't have access to either, use the blender method on page 15.

Rose water can be purchased from natural foods supermarkets like Whole Foods, or ethnic markets.

FUN FACT

Bartender Juan Coronado, who created this drink, says that it is one of his favorites, and when famed Spanish chef Ferran Adrià of elBulli tried it, even he asked for the recipe!

meet mezcal Think of tequila and mezcal as siblings. They're distilled from the same type of plant (agave), but tequila is made specifically from the Blue Agave species, whereas mezcal can be distilled from any type of agave. Interestingly, though, tequila and mezcal have completely different flavor profiles. While tequila can be smooth, clean, and vegetal, mezcal is earthy, funky, and smoky—which is why fans of smoky Scotch often enjoy mezcal.

Mezcal has a centuries-old history in Mexico, and while mezcal production is legally recognized in only eight states (meaning, producers in those regions can actually label their product "mezcal"), many other areas produce the spirit—and there it's referred to as an "agave spirit." Oaxaca, in southern Mexico, is considered mezcal's home.

WILDCARD COCKTAILS

Unexpected Liquors to Taste and Explore

The world of cocktails feels more exciting right now than perhaps ever before. Bartenders have more "toys" with which to play than they had in the past, be it a sous vide machine to impart flavor, liquid nitrogen to quickly chill a drink, or access to a *cidre* from Brittany that's only recently become available. When it comes to specific liquors, sherry is having a moment, as are amari, vermouth, and wine-based drinks made with Asian ingredients.

The influx of previously inaccessible or uncommon ingredients gives all of us the ability to make truly surprising and delicious drinks—no fancy equipment needed. In this chapter, you'll learn about alternative liquors like sake, shochu, and sherry that shouldn't be overlooked. These liquors lend themselves to a wide variety of cocktails, especially new takes on classics, from a martini to a caipirinha. But wait—don't skip this chapter out of fear of not being able to source these bottles! While they may sound unfamiliar, most are actually pretty easy to find at a local liquor store. (And of course, most ingredients are also just a click away.)

sakura
MARTINI

FROM **KENTA GOTO** OF **BAR GOTO, NEW YORK CITY**

J apan has one of the most meticulous cocktail cultures, and that attention to detail lends itself to beautifully flavored drinks with ornate garnishes. It often takes a bartender 15 minutes or longer to build just a single drink! Which is why I love this libation from Kenta Goto—owner of New York's Japanese-inspired Bar Goto—because it channels the flavors of Japan through a classically American libation. But here, Goto reimagines the traditionally boozy martini as a drink that's much lower in alcohol and easier on the palate. **MAKES 1**

2½ ounces sake

1 ounce gin (Kenta uses Plymouth)

¼ teaspoon maraschino liqueur

Cherry blossom or other edible flower, for garnish (optional)

1 Place a coupe or martini glass in the freezer to chill, 30 minutes.

2 Fill a mixing glass two-thirds full with ice cubes and add the sake, gin, and maraschino liqueur. Stir to chill well.

3 Strain into the chilled glass and garnish with the cherry blossom.

floating
FLOWER

FROM **RICHARD BREITKREUTZ** OF **IZI, NEW YORK CITY**

T here's something so elegant about this pale green cocktail. It captures a fresh green apple flavor with a floral undertone thanks to both the sake and elderflower liqueur. It's what you'd want to be drinking at a spa.

Make sure to use fresh celery juice here. If you don't have a juicer, you can blend fresh celery in a blender until it becomes a pulp, then pour that mixture through cheesecloth or a fine-mesh sieve and reserve the strained juice for the cocktail. Another option is to buy fresh celery juice from your local juice bar or a market like Whole Foods. The good news: You can juice a bunch of celery and it will keep in your fridge for 2 days. **MAKES 1**

2 ounces floral sake, such as Soto

1 ounce fresh celery juice (made from 1 bunch celery)

¾ ounce elderflower liqueur, such as St-Germain

½ ounce fresh lemon juice

Edible flower, for garnish

Combine the sake, celery juice, elderflower liqueur, and lemon juice in a cocktail shaker. Add ice cubes, cover, and shake to chill, 30 seconds. Strain into a coupe glass and garnish with the edible flower.

passion fruit
CAIPI-SANTI

O nce upon a time, I fell in love with a Brazilian man. We had a whirlwind romance in New York, and a month later he asked me to visit him in Brazil. There, I drank Brazil's national beverage, the caipirinha, on a daily basis, making sure to order mine spiked with fresh passion fruit juice. In the end I left my heart in Brazil (watch out for those Latin lovers!), but I returned home with a newfound affinity for the country's staple spirit, cachaça, and the know-how to build the perfect caipirinha. This recipe, which is sour-sweet and tastes of passion fruit and lime, is inspired by Brazil's exotic beauty, in low-ABV, sippable form.

A traditional caipirinha is composed of three simple ingredients: cachaça, lime, and white sugar. Because the drink is almost entirely flavored with lime (and any floral, fruity notes in the cachaça), it's vital to use super fresh limes, and that holds true for this recipe, too. In Brazil, you know how fresh the limes are? They're plucked moments before you drink them, directly off the trees. **MAKES 1**

½ lime, cut into six pieces (see box)

2 ounces sake

2 teaspoons sugar

1 fresh passion fruit, or 1 tablespoon defrosted frozen passion fruit pulp (see Note)

C ombine the lime, sake, sugar, and passion fruit in a cocktail shaker, and muddle together. Fill the shaker one-quarter full with crushed ice, cover, and shake until the shaker is frosty, about 15 seconds. Pour the drink (do not strain it) into an old-fashioned glass.

NOTE: It's super easy to prep passion fruit! Slice the fruit in half widthwise, then use a spoon to scoop out the yellow pulpy seeds (they're edible). Throw those right into your cocktail shaker.

Frozen passion fruit pulp is available in the freezer aisle of some supermarkets and online. I like the one made by Les Vergers Boiron.

it's all about technique What I learned in Brazil is that the trick to a great caipirinha is how you treat the lime. By that I mean, you need to cut it in a very specific way. First, slice off the ends of the lime so that the flesh shows. Next, cut the lime in half lengthwise. Now, here is the important part: Turn the lime cut-side up and, in a V-shape, cut out and discard the white core that runs lengthwise down the center. (That's how you prevent the drink from tasting bitter.) Next, place the lime cut-side down, halve it lengthwise, and slice it crosswise three times to make six equal pieces.

BEBIDAS

AGUAS WATERMELON-CILANTRO, LEMON-LIME-JICAMA — 6
COCO FRESH YOUNG THAI COCONUT — 6
REFRESCOS MEXICAN SODAS: COCA COLA, SQUIRT — 4
GRANADA DE PIÑA OUR FAMOUS PINEAPPLE BOMB! VIRGIN PIÑA COLADA WITH CHILI — 9

TACOS / 2 tacos per order

POLLO PULLED CHIPOTLE CHICKEN, PICKLED CABBAGE, AVOCADO CREMA — 11
CARNITAS SLOW ROASTED PORK SHOLDER, ONION, CILANTRO, SALSA VERDE — 12
CARNE ASADA NY STRIP STEAK PICKLED HOMINY, RED ONION, CREMA FRESCA — 12
ESCADO GRILLED DAILY FISH, RED CABBABGE, CITRUS CREMA — 12
ERDURAS ROASTED MARKET VEGETABLES, QUESO FRESCO, AVOCADO CREMA — 10

AÑAMIENTOS

GRILLED CORN ON THE COB, CHILE, QUESO FRESCO, LIME — 5
MERCADO MARKET GUACAMOLE, HOUSEMADE TORTILLA CHIPS — 8
RICE & BLACK BEANS, QUESO FRESCO, CREMA, PICO DE GALLO — 6

RES

MADE MEXICAN POPSICLES: DAILY FLAVORS — 5
USEMADE MEXICAN SOFT SERVE ICE CREAM: TWO DAILY FLAVORS — 6
SOFT SERVE ICE CREAM IN A HOUSEMADE CHURRO CONE — 7

ORIGINAL RESTAURANT & TEQUILA BAR!
RS STREET, NYC 10012 @PULQUERIANYC

the
BIG A

FROM **TONY ABOU-GANIM, LAS VEGAS**

N o! This is not a mocktail, but it sure tastes like one! Here, the flavor of fall comes through with a nod to the exotic in this shochu-based drink. The classic flavors of apple and a double hit of ginger marry in a highly refreshing low-proof cocktail that finishes with a hint of citrusy lemongrass and tastes totally devoid of booze. **MAKES 1**

½ ounce Kai Lemongrass Ginger Shochu (see Note and box)

¾ ounce ginger liqueur, such as Canton

2 ounces unfiltered apple juice (the cloudy kind)

1 ½ ounces Lemon Sour (recipe follows)

Chilled ginger ale

2 apple slices and lemon twist, for garnish

1 Combine the shochu, ginger liqueur, apple juice, and lemon sour in a cocktail shaker. Fill three-quarters full with ice cubes, cover, and shake to chill, about 15 seconds.

2 Fill a Collins glass with ice cubes and strain the shochu mixture into it. Top with ginger ale and stir gently to combine. Garnish with the apple slices and lemon twist.

NOTE: Kai Lemongrass Ginger Shochu is available online and at some liquor stores. If you can't find it, you can make your own using regular shochu. Simply trim and slice one stalk (6 to 8 inches long) of fresh lemongrass (see page 71), and place it in a 750-ml bottle of unflavored shochu. Let infuse for 4 days, then strain and discard the lemongrass. It will keep, covered in the refrigerator, for about 2 months.

meet shochu Japanese shochu—not to be confused with lower-proof Korean soju—is a clear liquor usually distilled from starches or grain that contains about 20 to 30 percent alcohol. That means it's lower in proof than a spirit, like vodka, but it's higher in booze than sake or grape wine. I like to think of shochu as a vodka replacement since its flavor is smooth, clean, and subtle.

Shochu was hot in London a few years back, but still has not broken through here in the States (possibly due to its similarity to vodka and the craft cocktail profession's view of vodka over the past several years). Slowly, however, more establishments are adopting the versatile liquor thanks to its lower ABV and the fact that it registers lower on the caloric chart as well.

lemon
SOUR

makes ¾ cup

½ cup fresh lemon juice

¼ cup Simple Syrup (page 26)

COMBINE THE LEMON JUICE WITH the simple syrup in a jar with a tight-fitting lid. Close the jar and shake to blend.

Lemon Sour will keep, covered and refrigerated, for about 1 week.

sherry
COBBLER

T hanks to the resurgence of speakeasies and a more recent rise in domestic sherry consumption, this classic nineteenth-century cocktail is finding its way back onto American bar menus. Built from sherry, simple syrup, and fruit, this drink can exist in countless variations based on available ingredients—have fun exploring the suggestions that follow. **MAKES 1**

• •

2 orange wheels

¼ ounce Simple Syrup (page 26) or more to taste

3 ounces amontillado sherry

• •

1 Muddle one orange wheel and the simple syrup in a cocktail shaker. Add the sherry and fill three-quarters full with ice cubes. Cover and shake until the shaker is frosty, about 15 seconds.

2 Pour the drink (do not strain it) into a highball glass filled with crushed ice and top with more crushed ice. Garnish with the remaining orange wheel.

FUN FACT

According to David Wondrich in his book *Imbibe!*, which explores the history of classic American cocktails, the sherry cobbler was once so popular that it's credited with introducing the public to two now-staple drink gadgets: the straw and the cocktail shaker.

variations

Try adding one of the following combinations to the muddle in step 1 of the Sherry Cobbler (page 185):

1 THE RAINES METHOD
2 strawberries + 2 blackberries

2 BERRY SERIOUS
3 raspberries + 4 blueberries

3 VANILLA COBBLER
¼ teaspoon pure vanilla extract

4 PINEAPPLE HOLIDAY
2 pineapple chunks (each about 1½ square inches and ½ inch thick)

5 CHERRY ON TOP
3 high-quality maraschino cherries, like Luxardo brand

JEREZANA

FROM **SHINGO GOKAN** OF **ANGEL'S SHARE, NEW YORK CITY**

Spaniards love their tonic water. After all, Spain's hometown hero is the gin and tonic, basically the country's national drink from Seville to San Sebastian. Gin-and-tonic bars are everywhere in Spain—with the drink often served in fishbowl-size goblets.

Here, Shingo Gokan, of New York's secret Japanese cocktail lounge Angel's Share, omits the gin and blends in another Spanish staple: sherry. What results is a super refreshing cocktail that skews sour thanks to the addition of sherry vinegar, with a subtle bitterness from the tonic. **MAKES 1**

• •

1 ounce Pedro Ximénez sherry	Tonic water
¼ ounce sherry vinegar	Orange wheel and fresh thyme sprig, for garnish

• •

Fill a Collins glass three-quarters full with ice cubes. Add the sherry and sherry vinegar, and stir to chill. Top with tonic water and garnish with the orange and thyme.

FUN FACT

One tonic water origin story links it to Spanish colonists in Peru, who made an antimalarial from the bitter bark of the cinchona tree—and mixed it with sugar to make it more palatable.

manzanilla
OLD FASHIONED

FROM **NICO DE SOTO** OF **MACE, NEW YORK CITY**

T his deceptively simple libation is incredibly delicious. Think nutty yet briny, with a hint of vanilla sweetness. A fun tip for the leftover vanilla syrup: Add it to coffee in place of sugar. **MAKES 1**

2 ounces Manzanilla sherry, such as La Garrocha

¼ ounce Vanilla Syrup (recipe follows)

2 dashes celery bitters, such as Fee Brothers

Orange peel, for garnish

1 Combine the sherry, vanilla syrup, and celery bitters in a mixing glass. Fill halfway with ice cubes and stir to chill.

2 Place a large ice cube in a rocks glass and strain the cocktail into it. Garnish with the orange peel.

vanilla
SYRUP

makes 1 ½ cups

1 cup water

1 cup sugar

1 vanilla bean, split in half lengthwise,
with the seeds scraped out

1 Combine the water, sugar, and vanilla bean pod and seeds in a small saucepan over medium heat and cook, stirring occasionally, until the sugar has dissolved, about 10 minutes. Remove from the heat and let cool.

2 Cover and let infuse at room temperature for 48 hours. Leave the vanilla bean in the syrup and use a funnel to transfer the syrup, and then bean, into an airtight container.

Vanilla Syrup will keep, covered and refrigerated, for about 1 week.

good evening, SPITFIRE

FROM **MEAGHAN DORMAN** OF **THE BENNETT, NEW YORK CITY**

Confession: Sometimes when I make cocktails at home and a recipe calls for a specific type of bitters that I don't have, I just leave it out. And usually the drink is still great. But with this recipe, the mole bitters really make a big difference. There's a cool chocolate note that comes through in this coconut drink, which celebrates all the flavors of Mexico: coconut, chile, mezcal, and cinnamon. I attribute that chocolate flavor to those essential mole bitters. **MAKES 1**

··

2½ ounces organic coconut milk

1½ ounces Ancho Reyes Chile Liqueur

½ ounce mezcal

1 teaspoon Cinnamon Syrup (recipe follows)

1 dash Bittermens Mole Bitters

Grated nutmeg (preferably fresh), for garnish

··

1 Fill a cocktail shaker with ice cubes. Add the coconut milk, chile liqueur, mezcal, cinnamon syrup, and bitters, cover, and shake to chill, about 10 seconds.

2 Place a large ice cube in a coffee mug and strain the cocktail into it. Sprinkle grated nutmeg on top.

....

cinnamon SYRUP

makes 2 cups

---

6 cinnamon sticks

2 cups sugar

1 cup water

COMBINE THE CINNAMON STICKS, SUGAR, and water in an airtight container, and stir to dissolve the sugar. Refrigerate overnight, then remove the cinnamon sticks.

Cinnamon Syrup will keep, covered and refrigerated, for about 2 weeks.

---

meet ancho reyes This spicy, ancho chile–infused liqueur is produced in Puebla, Mexico. It is 40 percent ABV.

saved
by the
BASIL

FROM **JOSH GOLDMAN** OF **BELCAMPO MEAT CO., LOS ANGELES**

S trawberries and basil are two ingredients I always associate with summer, and they are flavors that perfectly complement one another. This cocktail, which incorporates both, derives its sweetness from Dimmi, a peach-flavored Milanese liqueur infused with ingredients like rhubarb, orange peel, and peach blossoms. **MAKES 1**

• •

1 strawberry, hulled

1 ounce fino sherry, such as Valdespino Inocente

1 ounce Basilcello (recipe follows)

¾ ounce fresh lemon juice

½ ounce dry white vermouth, such as Dolin Dry

½ ounce Dimmi liqueur (see Note)

Lemon twist, for garnish

• •

1 Combine the strawberry, sherry, basilcello, lemon juice, dry vermouth, and Dimmi in a cocktail shaker, and muddle to break down the strawberry. Fill the shaker halfway with ice cubes, cover, and shake to chill, about 10 seconds.

2 Double-strain the cocktail into a coupe glass and garnish with the lemon twist.

NOTE: While there's nothing quite like Dimmi—a northern Italian aperitif liqueur that tastes of peaches—it can be tough to find (it's available at some liquor stores and online). If you can't get your hands on the stuff, try subbing in a sweet white vermouth like Dolin Blanc or double up on the dry vermouth.

variation

Feeling creative? Switch up the Dimmi for an equal amount of amaro like Meletti or an aperitif wine like Cocchi Aperitivo Americano. In place of floral peach notes, the cocktail will take on more savory herbal flavors.

If you want to cut down the booze content here further, try shaking the cocktail softly for 5 seconds (so that it's underdiluted), then strain the drink over ice into a Collins glass and top with soda water.

basilcello

makes 2¼ cups

¼ bunch (¼ pound) fresh basil leaves, washed

¾ cup high-proof neutral grain spirit,
such as Everclear (190 proof)

¾ cup water

1½ cups Simple Syrup (page 26)

1 Place the basil in a large nonreactive bowl (with a pouring spout, if you have one) and add the grain spirit. Cover the bowl and refrigerate to infuse the liquor, 24 hours.

2 Strain out and discard the basil. Stir the water and simple syrup into the infused liquor.

3 Using a funnel (and a ladle if the bowl doesn't have a spout), transfer the liquor mixture to a glass bottle or jar for serving and storage.

Basilcello will keep, covered and refrigerated, for about 3 months.

hangover
CURE

FROM **JUSTIN PIKE** of **THE TASTING KITCHEN, VENICE, CA**

A few years ago I found myself sitting at the bar of The Tasting Kitchen in Venice, California—one of my favorite restaurants in the city. I was hungover. Like, really hungover. Justin Pike, the wizard behind the eatery's excellent bar program, said he had a hangover remedy for me. I love this almost-mocktail because the spicy ginger calms the stomach while adding a refreshing peppery punch. The trifecta of cola, ginger ale, and bubbly water are what I crave now when I'm hungover. With the addition of savory, herbal, and minty fernet (one of many botanical-based amari, which centuries ago were consumed for their medicinal properties), the combination more than works! **MAKES 1**

....

½ ounce fernet

½ ounce fresh ginger juice
(see Note, page 163)

¼ ounce fresh lime juice

2 ounces club soda

1 ounce ginger ale

1 ounce Coke or
other cola

4 dashes Angostura bitters

Lime wedge, for garnish

....

Fill a Collins glass three-quarters full with ice cubes. Add the fernet, ginger juice, and lime juice, and stir together to combine. Slowly pour in the club soda, ginger ale, and Coke, one at a time, to achieve a layered look (do not mix). Top with the Angostura bitters and garnish with the lime wedge.

ginger, spice, and everything NICE

FROM **GINGER WARBURTON**, FORMERLY OF **VIRGINIA'S**, NEW YORK CITY

know I'm not supposed to pick favorites, but if I did, this cocktail would be at the top of my list. It is very easy to make: All you need to do is mix equal parts honey, ginger juice, and simple syrup, then add lemon and Byrrh, a beautiful aromatized wine. What you get is a ginger-forward cocktail, which—if you use a high-quality floral honey (I like orange blossom)—will be backed with a really pretty floral complexity. And I'd suggest using the leftover honey-ginger syrup in a quick mocktail. Just mix 1 cup of sparkling water with 1 ounce of syrup or more to taste. **MAKES 1**

¾ ounce fresh lemon juice

¾ ounce Honey-Ginger
Syrup (recipe follows)

2 ounces Byrrh (see box)

Lemon wheel, for garnish

F ill a cocktail shaker half full with ice cubes. Add the lemon juice, honey-ginger syrup, and Byrrh, cover, and shake to chill, about 10 seconds. Strain the cocktail into a rocks glass and garnish with the lemon wheel.

meet byrrh The French like to sip on bittersweet aperitif wines before dinner, and these wines are usually macerated with herbs that stimulate one's appetite. Byrrh falls into the aromatized aperitif wine category, and it's flavored with quinine—much like the original recipe for Lillet (see page 38)—a compound that comes from the bark of the cinchona tree.

honey-ginger
SYRUP

makes ¾ cup

¼ cup fresh ginger juice (see Note, page 163)

¼ cup honey

¼ cup Simple Syrup (page 26)

COMBINE THE GINGER JUICE, HONEY, and simple syrup in an airtight container, and stir until incorporated.

Honey-Ginger Syrup will keep, covered and refrigerated, for about 1 week.

into the
WOODS

FROM **LEO ROBITSCHEK** OF **THE NOMAD, NEW YORK CITY**

The Nomad, a wildly popular fine dining restaurant in Manhattan, is known for its excellent cocktails, and this drink is no exception. It is light and frothy thanks to the egg white, and the Douglas fir liqueur adds a sophisticated, floral, woodsy element that's accentuated by the vermouth. Understandably, raw egg whites in a drink might sound unappealing, but egg whites—which are basically flavorless—lend a silky mouthfeel to cocktails and also add a foamy cap.

On the subject of eggs and salmonella, I've never gotten sick from drinking an egg cocktail, but that's not to say that it can't happen. To minimize any risk, make sure your eggs are as fresh as possible. **MAKES 1**

½ ounce pure maple syrup

¾ ounce fresh lemon juice

1 ounce broVo Douglas fir liqueur (see Note)

1½ ounces sweet white vermouth, such as Dolin Blanc

1 egg white

Fresh rosemary sprig, for garnish

1 Combine the maple syrup, lemon juice, Douglas fir liqueur, vermouth, and egg white in a cocktail shaker, cover, and dry shake vigorously to emulsify the egg white, 10 seconds.

2 Add ice cubes to fill the shaker three-quarters full, cover, and shake a second time until the shaker is frosty, about 15 seconds. Strain the cocktail into a coupe glass and garnish with the rosemary sprig.

NOTE: This is a type of piney-flavored liqueur made in Washington that derives its taste from the Douglas fir tree. It can be purchased online.

BUZZ-FREE BEVERAGES

Mocktails in Which You Don't Miss the Booze

Sometimes you crave a delicious, refreshing drink minus the buzz. Perhaps you're at lunch with a co-worker, are attending (or the guest of honor at) a baby shower, or are refueling before a workout. A few years ago, I noticed a trend of restaurants serving artisanal sodas as alcohol-free beverage options, but more recently chefs have begun to take their beverage programs more seriously, adding creative drinks to their menu using house-made flavored syrups and fresh juices—just like cocktails, but without any booze. Some tasting-menu restaurants across the country have even added an entire beverage-pairing option composed of mocktails, for those staying away from the hard stuff. Truth of the matter is, mocktails—when thoughtfully composed—can be just as great as cocktails; the drinks in this chapter won't even make you miss the booze.

If you're the designated driver tonight, read on!

beet
WINE

FROM **EAMON ROCKEY, NEW YORK CITY**

Bar wizard Eamon Rockey, formerly of Betony in New York City, inspired America's milk punch craze, and his drink list spans the gamut from riffs on classics to cocktails that require three weeks of prep. Eamon's drink program at Betony was crazy cool, and it was one that didn't overlook the mocktail. Here, Eamon creates a smart red wine replacement using just fruit, veg, and tea. When served in a wineglass, it's almost jarring how much the drink looks like red wine. I use a juicer to make the apple and beet juices, but you can also use a blender (see box, page 15). Or stop by your local juice bar and ask them to make the apple and beet juices for you up to a day in advance. **MAKES 1**

1½ Granny Smith apples (to yield 5 ounces juice)

1 red beet (to yield 2 ounces juice)

4 ounces double-strength oolong tea, chilled (see Note)

1 Using a juicer or blender, juice the apples (core them first if using a blender). Transfer the juice to a glass jar with a lid. Juice the beet and transfer the juice to a separate glass jar with a lid. Place the juices in the refrigerator overnight to rest and allow the solids to settle to the bottom.

2 Strain each juice through cheesecloth to remove any sediment. Combine the strained apple and beet juices and the tea in a pitcher. Chill until ready to serve.

3 Before serving, skim off any foam or solids floating on top, and decant off of the settled solids at the bottom. Serve in wineglasses.

Beet Wine will keep, covered and refrigerated, for up to 4 days.

NOTE: To make double-strength tea, just double the amount of tea leaves you would ordinarily use. If you're using tea bags, use two instead of one. If you have loose-leaf tea, go with 2 teaspoons of tea leaves to 1 cup of water (unless the leaves are balled up, in which case use 1 teaspoon).

Add ½ ounce grappa.

gingered lemon
HOT TODDY

FROM **AMANDA CHANTAL BACON** OF **MOON JUICE,**
VENICE, CA

J uice witch Amanda Chantal Bacon operates the best juice bars in Los Angeles under the Moon Juice name. There, you'll find curative tonics and elixirs, similar to the recipe here. This tart combination of apples, lemons, and apple cider vinegar gets a boost of heat from both the fresh ginger and cayenne, making it the perfect hot drink during cooler temperatures, especially in the fall when apples are in season.

This recipe calls for a juicer. If you don't have one, you can use the blender method on page 15 to juice the lemons and apples and the box grater method on page 163 for the ginger (or—even easier—use bottled ginger juice). **MAKES 3**

3 Granny Smith apples, halved

2½ lemons, peeled and halved

One 3-inch piece fresh ginger (to yield ½ ounce juice)

1 tablespoon apple cider vinegar

Pinch cayenne pepper

1 Pass the apples, lemons, and ginger through a juicer. (If using a blender, peel and core the apples and peel, seed, and quarter the lemons before placing in the blender along with ½ ounce ginger juice.)

2 Transfer the juice to a medium-size saucepan over medium heat. Add the vinegar and cayenne pepper and cook, stirring occasionally, until it's just simmering, about 4 minutes.

3 Pour into mugs and serve.

Add ½ ounce whiskey.

sugar plum
TONIC

FROM **MARIE ZAHN** OF **BUTCHERTOWN GROCERY, LOUISVILLE, KY**

I n a cocktail, bitters act like a seasoning (similar to how chefs use salt and pepper to amplify the flavors of a dish). The fun part about bitters, depending on the ingredients in a given bottle, is that they're an easy way to add underlying flavor and boost a drink's complexity with just a couple of dashes. Here, they're used in what is essentially a grown-up lemonade thanks to the tonic water and the softest suggestion of spice. **MAKES 1**

¾ ounce fresh lemon juice

¾ ounce Simple Syrup (page 26)

2 dashes Fee Brothers Plum Bitters

2 ounces tonic water, chilled

Lemon twist, for garnish

1 Fill a cocktail shaker three-quarters full with ice cubes. Add the lemon juice, simple syrup, and bitters and cover. Shake to chill, about 10 seconds. Add the tonic water.

2 Strain the liquid into a coupe glass and garnish with the lemon twist.

Add ½ shot of vodka.

strawberry yuzu green tea TONIC

FROM **MELINA MEZA** OF **INK., LOS ANGELES**

A shrub—very different from the bush growing in your front yard—is essentially a fruit-and-vinegar–based drink that was popular in eighteenth- and nineteenth-century America, especially among farmworkers toiling under the hot sun. In the past few years, this ancient drink (and the syrup that acts as its foundation and shares its name) have made a modern comeback. Its beauty lies in its acidic vinegary punch, which heightens the supporting flavors. In this case, both lemon and yuzu highlight the strawberry, while the tonic chimes in with a bitter balance.

Note the strawberry shrub syrup recipe yields more than necessary for one cocktail. Keep it in your fridge and add a shot to a glass of club soda for a quick refreshment. **MAKES 1**

1 ½ ounces Strawberry Shrub Syrup (recipe follows)

1 ounce brewed green tea, preferably sencha, chilled

¾ ounce fresh lemon juice

¼ ounce yuzu juice (or additional lemon juice in a pinch)

Tonic water

Lemon wheel, for garnish

Combine the strawberry shrub syrup, green tea, lemon juice, and yuzu juice in a pint glass. Add ice cubes and stir. Top with tonic water and garnish with the lemon wheel.

Booze It Up

Add ½ ounce gin.

strawberry
SHRUB SYRUP

makes about 3 cups

---

1 cup sugar

1 cup water

½ pint strawberries, rinsed and hulled

1 cup red verjus (see Note, page 52)

---

1 Combine the sugar and water in a medium-size saucepan over low heat and cook, stirring occasionally, until the sugar has dissolved, 3 minutes.

2 Add the strawberries. Turn up the heat to medium-high and cook until the mixture begins to boil, then reduce the heat to medium-low and simmer for 5 minutes.

3 Strain the syrup through a sieve over an airtight container and discard the strawberries (or eat them later over yogurt!). Let the syrup cool. Stir in the verjus.

Strawberry Shrub Syrup will keep, covered and refrigerated, for 1 week.

nuts in a
VICE

FROM **VINCENZO MARIANELLA** OF **LOVE & SALT,**
MANHATTAN BEACH, CA

ne of Los Angeles's original cocktail ninjas, Vincenzo Marianella has earned a reputation as one of the city's leading bartenders serving fresh cocktails made with seasonal ingredients. Here, Vincenzo creates what almost tastes like a mild, carbonated Creamsicle that's refreshed with a hint of mint. **MAKES 1**

10 to 15 fresh mint leaves

¾ ounce fresh lime juice

¾ ounce almond syrup
(see Note)

2 ounces fresh orange juice

3 ounces soda water

Mint sprig and thin orange wheel, for garnish

Combine the mint leaves, lime juice, almond syrup, orange juice, and soda water in a highball glass, and stir gently. Add crushed ice to fill the glass. Garnish with the mint sprig and orange wheel.

NOTE: For this mocktail, Vincenzo uses a brand of almond syrup called Monin, which you can easily find online. But you can also make your own using the orgeat recipe on page 28. Orgeat is a toasted almond syrup often used in cocktails. I've also made this drink with almond milk in place of the almond syrup, and it's still quite tasty. If your almond milk is unsweetened, you'll want to add sugar to taste.

Add ½ ounce dark rum.

jasmine
LIMEADE

T his recipe—perfect for kids—was born from a variety of inspirations: (1) A year ago in Austin, Texas, at a restaurant called Elizabeth, I tried a great take on lemonade, imbued with the flavor of jasmine tea. (2) Having recently returned from Brazil where lime typically replaces lemon, I decided to swap out the lemon for lime (though either fruit works). (3) And finally, one of my favorite summertime activities as a kid was running a lemonade stand. Lemonade is the ultimate kid-friendly thirst quencher. If you're going to garnish such a mocktail, obviously rainbow sprinkles are essential! **MAKES 1**

••

1 cup water

1 teaspoon jasmine tea leaves

½ tablespoon honey

½ cup rainbow sprinkles, for garnish

Lime or lemon wheel, for garnish

4 teaspoons fresh lime juice (or 3 teaspoons fresh lemon juice)

••

1 Place the water in a small saucepan over medium heat and bring to a simmer.

2 Add the jasmine tea leaves, then turn off the heat. Let the tea leaves steep, about 3 minutes, then taste the tea. If there's not enough jasmine flavor, steep for another 1 or 2 minutes (be careful not to oversteep as jasmine leaves quickly become tannic).

3 Add the honey and stir to combine. Strain the tea through a fine-mesh sieve and discard the leaves. Allow the tea to cool.

4 Pour the sprinkles onto a small plate or into a shallow bowl. Run the lime wheel along the rim of a clear plastic Dixie cup to moisten it. Dip the rim of the cup into the sprinkles to coat.

5 Fill the prepared cup three-quarters full with ice cubes, add the tea mixture and lime juice, and stir to combine. Garnish with the lime wheel.

Add ½ shot of gin or vodka.

CONVERSION TABLES

1 cup sugar = 8 oz = 220 g
1 cup (firmly packed)
   brown sugar =
   6 oz = 220 g to 230 g

1 cup confectioners' sugar =
   4½ oz = 115 g
1 cup honey or syrup = 12 oz

BASIC BAR TOOL CONVERSIONS

½ ounce = 1 tablespoon =
   3 teaspoons
¾ ounce = 4½ teaspoons
1 ounce = 2 tablespoons =
   6 teaspoons

1½ ounces = 3 tablespoons
2 ounces = ¼ cup =
   4 tablespoons
Dash = ⅛ to 1/16 teaspoon
Splash = ½ teaspoon

LIQUID CONVERSIONS

U.S.	IMPERIAL	METRIC
1 teaspoon or bar spoon	⅛ fluid ounce	4 ml
1 tablespoon	½ fluid ounce	15 ml
2 tablespoons	1 fluid ounce	30 ml
3 tablespoons	1½ fluid ounces	45 ml
¼ cup	2 fluid ounces	60 ml
⅓ cup	2½ fluid ounces	75 ml
½ cup	4 fluid ounces	125 ml
⅔ cup	5 fluid ounces	150 ml
¾ cup	6 fluid ounces	175 ml
1 cup	8 fluid ounces	250 ml
2 cups (1 pint)	16 fluid ounces	500 ml
1 quart	32 fluid ounces	0.95 liter

INDEX

Note: Page references in *italics* indicate photographs.